HGreater ARTFORD

CELEBRATING CULTURAL DIVERSITY

By Jim H. Smith

Photography by Lanny Nagler

LONGSTREET PRESS
Atlanta, Georgia

PUBLISHED IN COOPERATION WITH
THE GREATER HARTFORD CHAMBER OF COMMERCE

Published by
LONGSTREET PRESS
a subsidiary of Cox Newspapers
a subsidiary of Cox Enterprises, Inc.
2140 Newmarket Parkway
Suite 118
Marietta, Georgia 30067

Published in cooperation with the
Greater Hartford Chamber of Commerce
250 Constitution Plaza
Hartford, Connecticut 06103

Printed in the United States of America

1st printing, 1996
Library of Congress
Catalog Number 95-77263

ISBN: 1-56352-267-5

This book was printed by
Quebecor/Kingsport, Tennessee.

Color separation and film preparation
by Advertising Technologies, Inc.
Atlanta, Georgia

DIRECTOR, ENTERPRISE DIVISION
Nancy Bauer

MANAGING EDITOR
Erica Fox

ART DIRECTION AND PRODUCTION
Graham & Company Graphics, Inc.
Atlanta, Georgia

CONTENTS

FOREWORD

I was delighted when I was asked to write this foreword to *Greater Hartford: Celebrating Cultural Diversity*.

A new spirit has been born in Hartford and the Greater Hartford area. In every corner of the region, Greater Hartford is building for a bold new future. From Hartford's neighborhoods to its neighboring towns and cities, from the businesses to the arts and entertainment community, to Greater Hartford's outstanding health-care and educational institutions, exciting new projects are in development.

We want people to share that excitement. We want people to see what the Greater Hartford region has to offer. *Greater Hartford: Celebrating Cultural Diversity* is a great way to help us tell the story of the magical things going on here.

This book tells the story of how Hartford is recapturing the Connecticut River. It offers insight into why Hartford's Arts and Entertainment District is growing by leaps and bounds. It takes the reader on a guided tour of Hartford's vibrant, multicultural neighborhoods. It reviews remarkable changes going on in the region's top-notch universities and health-care institutions. And it explores the promise of increasing collaboration between those institutions.

Most of all, *Greater Hartford: Celebrating Cultural Diversity* is the inspiring story of the diverse people who live in the Greater Hartford area and contribute to our remarkably rich blend of cultures and heritages. That diversity is one of our greatest strengths, and in vibrant photographs and text, this book brings Greater Hartford and its people to life for the reader.

I hope you'll enjoy reading *Greater Hartford: Celebrating Cultural Diversity*. And after you've read it, I welcome you to visit Greater Hartford. Whether you're looking for a vacation option, a place to hold your next convention or conference, or a place to build your business, I promise that you'll find what you're looking for here.

MAYOR MIKE PETERS
CITY OF HARTFORD

A WORD FROM THE PHOTOGRAPHER

he journey to this point has been a long one, not only in miles traveled during the past four months but in the way my perception of Greater Hartford has changed as I took the photographs for this book.

Like many of you, I was guilty of the common misconception that "there is nothing going on in Hartford." Nothing could be further from the truth. What I came to realize was that I would be able to capture only a small sample of what is going on here.

Every day I would pick up the paper and read about a multitude of places or events that I knew I couldn't get to visit. What you see in these photos is just the tip of the iceberg. I only hope that after you have looked through this book, it doesn't become part of your coffee table. Instead, I encourage you to motivate yourself to get out and experience what I have discovered is a fabulous city and region.

Whenever possible, I have tried to give a unique perspective—whether it was backstage at the Hartford Ballet, down on the field at a Coyotes game, flying down the Connecticut River on a bass boat, or watching the sun set on Hartford from the top of Goodwin Square.

The physical beauty and events are only a part of the story, though. At the center are the people of Greater Hartford. Some I met only briefly. With others, I spent hours. Not one person denied my request to be photographed. That had never happened before—anywhere.

This is a region of warm and open people. Everywhere I went, I was welcomed—by the kids and community leaders at Blue Hills Family Day, by the proud residents of the Park Street community during Parkfest, and by the many people I met in Hartford's suburbs. I had the cooperation of everyone I asked for a favor—whether it was to gain access to an event or to climb a precipitous height.

There are too many people to thank individually, but I am eternally grateful for their help. I would, however, especially like to thank my family for their patience and understanding. I would also like to thank Jim Smith for his collaborative spirit and sense of humor and my assistant, Holly Augeri, for her insight and positive attitude.

In the final analysis, my hope is twofold. For those of you who live in the Greater Hartford area, I hope this book gives you pride in the place you call home. For those who have a role in shaping the future course for this region, I trust that it inspires you to continue with even greater vigor and optimism.

Late morning, April 20, 1995. A pretty day.

As winters go, we haven't had a bad one. But it has been tenacious and, throughout March and the early weeks of April, mean-spirited. It has hung on and hung on, repeatedly teasing us with tastes of warm weather, only to return with strings of raw, blustery days.

But this morning feels authentic—like real spring. And my eight-year-old son, Ryland, and I are going for a plane ride. We have bought a half hour of time from Million Air, a flight school and charter service based at Brainard Airport in Hartford's South End.

"This is research," I tell the pilot before we leave the ground. "I'm writing a book about the Greater Hartford area. I want to see what Hartford looks like from above."

"Sure," the pilot says accommodatingly. "I can show you Hartford."

The book is supposed to celebrate diversity. It pivots on the dual notions that Hartford and the area around it are poised for a renaissance and that somehow this rebirth will be the consequence of the region's rich diversity.

Ryland is eager to get in the air, but I'm thinking I probably won't learn much about diversity from a quarter of a mile above Hartford. Still, it seems like as good a place as any to start. After all, you can't get to the details without grasping the big picture.

The pilot's name is Joe Nadeau. He's a good-looking, red-headed kid from that big sprawl across the Connecticut River that people locally refer to as the East Side.

With some guys, when you meet them, you know right away that they're doing exactly what they're supposed to do. Joe may have been a bird in another life.

■ ■ ■

We cross the sticky asphalt to the plane. It's a Cessna 172—a single-engine training plane with room for three people.

I climb in the back with my camera. My boy sits up front with Joe. We taxi out onto the runway and Joe talks briefly to the tower. Then we take off.

Within minutes we've climbed to cruising altitude. We're headed north above East Hartford when Joe turns the plane left to cross the Connecticut River and make our first sweep around Hartford.

From 1,500 feet up, I'm surprised to discover that you can see the silt bars on the bed of the Connecticut River. You can also see the concrete base of the extension of Constitution Plaza as it reaches the river, straddling I-91 and reconnecting Hartford with its aquatic heritage for the first time in some 60 years.

Across the river, along the shore of East Hartford, more construction is under way. Near the future site of the Science Museum of Connecticut, workers are constructing an outdoor theater.

I snap a few shots of this riverside development. It is one of the sites I hoped to see, and evidence of something new and vital growing from the rich soil of this ancient floodplain.

"Can you see the Meadows Music Theatre?" I ask. It's the new indoor-outdoor amphitheater under construction in Hartford's North Meadows area.

"Sure," says Joe. He turns the plane to the right and we loop back over the industrial buildings and railroad tracks of the North End.

"I've been watching this all spring," he says. "Something changes every day."

Not surprising. It's New England's first new major concert venue in years, and when it opens this summer, it's expected to attract thousands of music fans to Hartford for concerts year-round. Well before the project is complete, prominent national artists like Jimmy Buffett and R.E.M. are being booked.

Joe circles the construction site twice and then takes the plane south into a broad loop around Hartford. We turn above the state capitol, its gilded dome gleaming in the sun. Bushnell Park lies at the capitol's feet, a small green carpet.

I can see all the landmarks of Hartford: CityPlace, the Traveler's Tower, the Gold Building, the Wadsworth Atheneum, the Old State House, its renovation still a year from completion. I can see the construction that will be the new Connecticut Children's Medical Center, and more construction going on at Saint Francis Hospital and Medical Center. What's being built, I will soon discover, is not just new health-care facilities but the foundation for a new regional industry.

Now that I'm facing east, I can see the river in context. Rolling down from the north, it crooks an elbow here as it slouches toward the picturesque old villages that line its tidal banks in those last miles before it empties into Long Island Sound. It is a beautiful river, wide and leisurely, like the mid-Hudson.

This spring morning, with the sun glinting off its surface, the river is deceptively quiet. But I know it can be a monster. Nearly every year since I've lived here, it has flooded portions of Middletown and other villages downstream. Yet, to this day, some six decades since Hartford last relied upon it commercially, the river that clearly accounts for Hartford being where it is remains navigable to the ocean.

Joe turns northward again and we repeat our circumnavigation of downtown. I snap a few more pictures, surprised at how little you can tell about Hartford's neighborhoods from up here. Houses upon houses, they simply spread away from downtown in all directions.

If you can't identify the streets from the perspective of the birds, you can't tell where you are. There are no apparent lines of demarcation between Hartford and West Hartford, between West Hartford and Newington. There are just houses and trees. Parks. Ball fields. Golf courses. Schools. Gravel pits. Quarries. Shopping centers. Low-rise industrial buildings.

We aim west, following the beeline of Farmington Avenue, and Joe lets Ryland take the stick. This is a big deal for an eight-year-old, and he rises to the occasion. What he has to do is watch the instrument panel and keep the plane level on a horizon line. Child of the video game age, he does a commendable job.

Suburbia flows below us as we fly toward Avon and the bony spine that angles northwest across Connecticut from the Traprock region of Meriden on up through the hill country of Litchfield and into the Berkshires. We cross over the network of suburban reservoirs and hiking trails maintained by the Metropolitan District and turn back, our half hour nearly spent.

I write the word "possibilities" in the notebook I purchased for this assignment and underline it. I put an exclamation point after it. It is the only word I've written in the notebook so far.

Connecticut was severely pounded by the recession, and Hartford has had some difficulty rebounding. But this spring morning I have seen new life emerging here, and I'm a believer in cycles.

Joe banks the plane over Wethersfield Cove and levels off for our descent. "Did you see everything you were looking for?" he asks.

"Only some of it," I tell him. "The rest I need to find down here."

I'm not entirely certain what it is I'm looking for. The magic inherent in diversity? Things you can find only in the human heart?

Over the next few weeks I will look for those things throughout the Greater Hartford area. I will talk to artists and teachers, law enforcement officers and government officials, bartenders, architects and administrators, businesspeople and children.

I will visit places I've never heard of, in corners of the Greater Hartford region I've never visited before. I will write thousands of words and throw a lot of them away.

This is the story of what I learned. It is a story about a place, and so, like any such story, it is a story about the people who live there. It is a story about their dreams and visions.

Most of all, it is a story about hope.

Riverfront
Recapture

*H*artford resident Lee Bailey, Jr., shown on the
Connecticut River, has been a professional bass
fisherman for more than a decade.

In September 1994, the largest crowds in the history of the BASSMASTER Top 100 fishing tournament were not standing around a lake in Florida or the Ozarks.

No, the crowds were lining the riverfront in Hartford and East Hartford to watch some of America's foremost anglers take to the Connecticut River. The fishermen were lured by the promise of fish that wouldn't have dreamed of swimming in this water just a few years ago and by the prospect of more than $270,000 in cash and awards. It was the first time the prestigious tournament had been held anywhere in the Northeast. But it's not likely to be the last.

That's because the participants discovered what a lot of people are discovering. The Connecticut River is a lot better than it used to be. As Dewey Kendrick, head of the national B.A.S.S. organization, put it, "Y'all got a great river."

■   ■   ■

It *is* a great river. And if you're trying to get a bead on the future of this region, you quickly realize the story starts, like many great stories, on the waterfront.

In every true sense, the remarkable stream the Algonquins called Long River is an artery. The blood that originally gave life to Greater Hartford flowed through it. And the blood that can revitalize the local economy as we move into the 21st century flows through it now.

Born of springs and lakes far north in the rugged hills of New Hampshire, the river flows more than 400 miles before emptying into Long Island Sound. Along the way it serves as a border between New Hampshire and Vermont and bisects Massachusetts and Connecticut.

In its annual rebirth each spring, fed by the melting snow on hard granite mountains named after presidents, the river asserts itself in blind, youthful fury as it rips through narrow gorges. But by the time it reaches Saybrook and Old Lyme, it is a fat old folk song of a river, half a mile wide.

Fed by tributaries with ancient names like Nulhegan, Ottoquechee, and Ammonoosuc, the river has drained a watershed of more than 13,000 square miles, the largest in New England. It drifts through its final stretches at a steady, unhurried pace, rich in history and fish.

By regional standards, the Connecticut is a big river. And in Hartford it's about to have a big future.

■   ■   ■

$10.5 million!

That's the amount of money contributed to the local economy during the past few years by events tied to the river. Events like the BASSMASTER tournament, regional fishing tournaments, and major triathlons that involved swims in water only recently thought to be too polluted ever to recover.

It's serious money. But it's just a drop in the bucket, so to speak, compared with the potential.

No one speaks more eloquently about what the river can mean for Greater Hartford than Joe Marfuggi, the tireless promoter who heads Riverfront Recapture, Inc. Riverfront Recapture is a private, nonprofit organization created in 1981 by a group of corporate, civic,

$\mathcal{T}$hrough a program sponsored by Riverfront Recapture, Inc., inner-city youngsters are learning how to build boats. Their instructor, David R. Gilroy, has set up a "classroom" in Hartford's Main Street Market.

and political leaders who dreamed of making the river part of Greater Hartford's daily life once again. Their dream is about to become reality.

"This is going to be such an exciting place!" Marfuggi tells the passengers on a cruise of the *Lady Fenwick,* the tour boat that takes people up and down the river from Charter Oak Landing, the major recreational dock in Hartford's South End. Outlining the ambitious string of waterfront improvements that will unite Hartford and East Hartford before the turn of the century, he says, "The BASSMASTER tournament offers a preview of what will happen here regularly. The fact that tournament planners would even consider bringing the event to the Connecticut River is solid evidence that the quality of the water has improved dramatically in recent years."

"It's not an accident that Hartford and East Hartford are here," says Robert DeCrescenzo, mayor of East Hartford and another big booster of the river. "The river used to be this region's primary source of commerce and shipping. It was a natural part of everyone's daily life.

"There was a time when people routinely strolled between Hartford and East Hartford. There was a real sense of connectedness between the two cities. I believe the revitalization of our riverfront can help bring that back."

What happened? The answer, ironically, is progress.

Though the river was integral to Hartford's early economic life, it was also a killer. The city is built on the Connecticut's floodplain, and the flip side of the economic vitality was the potential for disaster.

After downtown Hartford was flooded in 1936 and 1938, city fathers decided enough was enough. By then, Hartford's economy was heavily invested in the burgeoning insurance industry that had grown rapidly after the Civil War. If building dikes to keep the rampaging river at bay meant relinquishing the city's traditional economic base, it seemed a small price to pay.

As if that wasn't enough of a barrier to put between the people of Hartford and the river, Interstate Highways 91 and 84, constructed in the 1960s and 1970s, sealed the deal. Suddenly, no one approached the river, because no one could.

■ ■ ■

Now, almost 60 years after flood walls were built with the best of intentions, and a quarter of a century after the modernist vision of an interstate highway system, construction that seems almost magical in its ingenuity is about to give the river back to the people.

In December 1994, after new highway lanes were built at ground level, construction crews removed an elevated section of I-91 in Hartford, the last big obstacle to completion of the riverfront project. Builders were free to move forward with the centerpiece of Riverfront Recapture's dream.

By 1997, a landscaped esplanade will extend downtown Hartford's Constitution Plaza across I-91, a railroad line, and the 60-year-old flood-control wall. A set of grassy terraces will descend to the river, creating amphitheater seating for some 2,000 people to enjoy concerts and other events.

At the same time, after Founders Bridge is completely rebuilt, a 15-foot-wide pedestrian promenade will make it possible for people to once more stroll from Hartford to East Hartford.

During a morning stroll along the river, one might see the tall ship Mystic Clipper, *out of Bath, Maine, tied up at Charter Oak Landing or students in a rowing class offered by Go Row, Hartford! preparing to embark.*

"WE'RE BUILDING ON INITIATIVES TO IMPROVE WATER QUALITY AND CREATE PUBLIC RECREATIONAL FACILITIES ALONG THE BANKS OF A RIVER THAT'S CLEANER AND MORE INVITING THAN IT'S BEEN IN GENERATIONS."

—JOE MARFUGGI, EXECUTIVE DIRECTOR, RIVERFRONT RECAPTURE, INC.

When the entire project is complete, people in Hartford will be able to cross Constitution Plaza, descend to the riverfront, and walk along the river as far south as Wethersfield and as far north as Riverside Park. Or they may elect to cross the river on the promenade and hike through East Hartford's Great River Park, site of another new outdoor amphitheater, with seating for several hundred.

Farther downriver, past the current boat launch, they will be able to enter a new extension of Great River Park embracing the proposed site of the Science Center of Connecticut. Finally, they will be able to return to Hartford by crossing the Charter Oak Bridge.

What will happen when all of this construction is complete is anyone's guess, but Marfuggi is quick to assert that merely building this network of parks will not be enough. "It must be well maintained," he says, "and exciting things must happen here." Marfuggi has a clear idea of what those things must be.

In his view, the completed riverfront project is a cornerstone of the current vision of Greater Hartford born anew as a diversified entertainment center. He can close his eyes and see a vibrant new waterfront where the two cities are connected not only by pedestrian bridges but by water taxis and commuter boats. He can see exciting events and entertainment venues springing up here, as well.

Most of all, in this incarnation, the river on which Billy Joel filmed his *River of Dreams* video presents Hartford and its neighboring communities with limitless opportunities for economic rebirth. In fact, early in 1995, the American Rivers organization gave its first economic revitalization award to Riverfront Recapture.

"Already the nation is noticing our new riverfront," Marfuggi says. "We're building on initiatives to improve water quality and create public recreational facilities along the banks of a river that's cleaner and more inviting than it's been in generations.

"That will mean more and bigger events, attracting greater numbers of competitors and spectators from across the nation. Economic development will follow on land adjacent to the lively new riverfront, outside the floodplain. And that will create new jobs and generate new tax revenue."

River Recapture may do even more than that. In a region that was severely beaten by the recession at the end of the 1980s, this project may be a powerful symbol of possibilities—an inspiration and a reminder that often we are the product of our own expectations.

In 1972, in the foreword to a book called *The Connecticut River*, former Connecticut senator Abraham Ribicoff wrote, "Time is running out for the Connecticut River. It would be sad to see a valley which survived man's ravages for over 300 years destroyed just when the nation is waking up to the many threats faced by our natural resources."

Twenty years later, and much cleaner, the river keeps on rolling. Now, suddenly, it is alive with possibility. And the citizens of the Greater Hartford area are about to get a new shot at being its stewards and a new shot at the future.

Above: Joe Marfuggi, executive director of Riverfront Recapture, Inc. *Right:* Cathedral-like arches support the Charter Oak Bridge between Hartford and East Hartford.

DOWN BY THE RIVER

The little kid with the glow stick around his neck sits on his dad's shoulders, watching the ocean of people ebb and flow across Constitution Plaza. He is lapping an ice cream cone, but he isn't working at it very hard. The crowd keeps diverting his attention.

There are, after all, 100,000-plus people, maybe more than he has ever seen before in one place. And up there on his father's shoulders, he is taller than all of them. So the ice cream keeps melting down over his fingers and dripping on his dad's hair.

A lot of these people were drawn to this year's Riverfest by reports that the fireworks display would be one of the most spectacular ever. It has been promoted as an extravaganza featur-ing innovative explosives designed by Atlas Advanced Pyrotechnics, the 1994 winner of the North American Fireworks Competition.

But now people are wondering if the fireworks are going to happen. The fire marshal, some speculate, won't allow them. It is raining too hard. The Hartford Symphony Orchestra, which was supposed to accompany the fire-works with stirring renditions of the *1812 Overture* and lots of John Philip Sousa chestnuts, is nowhere in sight.

As the evening's headliner, popular singer Chris Isaak, leaves the stage, someone across the river launches a couple of desultory rockets that arc briefly and fizzle out. No one is sure what's going to happen.

Finally, the loudspeakers crackle and an announcer on Constitution Plaza tells the crowd the show is on. The symphony isn't going to make it, but the musicians have prerecorded the requisite material.

Five minutes pass. The music starts. A few rockets go up. Then a pause.

And then, suddenly, the sky explodes and keeps right on exploding for the next half hour. Unending cascades and blossoms of shimmering light assault the night sky, and massive percussions ricochet off the walls of the surrounding buildings.

As the final notes of *Stars and Stripes Forever* end and echo off down the river, the crowd issues a collective sigh. Can there be any experience more primally satisfying than Riverfest's annual fire-works blowout? Maybe dribbling ice cream all over your dad's hair.

The river beckons sailors and fishermen of all ages. Right, a regatta sails past the historic Colt Armory, with its distinctive blue "onion," while in Riverside Park a budding angler learns the finer points of casting during Take a Kid Fishing Day.

*Y*oungsters enjoy a wide range of recreational activities on the increasingly clean Connecticut River.

*T*he Hartford skyline seen from East Hartford's Great River Park.

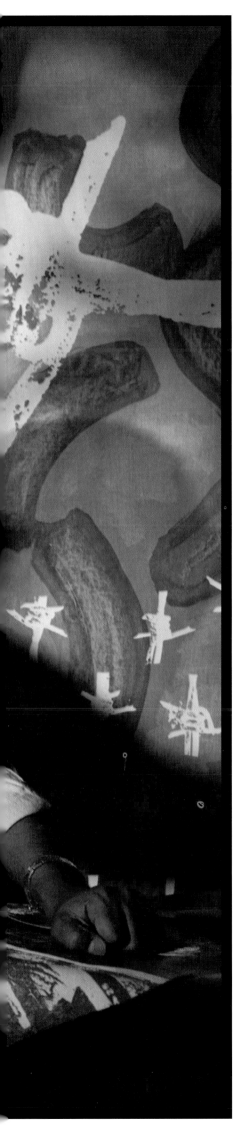

CONNECT THE DOTS:
HARTFORD'S ARTS AND ENTERTAINMENT DISTRICT

West Hartford resident Carlos Hernandez
Chavez is a painter and a musician.

*A*bove: Greater Hartford Arts Council volunteers clown around in the Arts and Entertainment District during the debut of Hartford's novel Connect the Dots program. Right: The Hartford Symphony.

e want Hartford to become the best community for arts and entertainment in the world," reads a brochure produced by the Greater Hartford Arts Council to celebrate its silver anniversary.

An ambitious goal? You bet. But these are exciting times for Greater Hartford's arts and entertainment community. Indeed, the council may very well have selected the most propitious window of time in the past 30 years to launch its plan.

If no one is exactly sure how to help Hartford reach its goal, there is no shortage of ideas and talent. These days, Hartford is wall to wall with impresarios. The strategy being promoted by the Arts Council is called Connect the Dots.

■   ■   ■

"Many people are not aware of what this region has to offer," says Robb Hankins, executive director of the Greater Hartford Arts Council, "the theaters, museums, historical sites, and concert halls that regularly entertain and delight hundreds of thousands of people annually."

Indeed, the council's regional arts inventory lists more than 150 organizations in Greater Hartford. To increase awareness of this resource, in 1994, the council, working with the Hartford City Council, designated a 20-block area of downtown Hartford as the city's official Arts and Entertainment District. The region's new identity as an arts and entertainment mecca is evolving from the collective success of the venues clustered in this 20-block area.

Included here are some of the country's most prestigious arts facilities, according to Prentice Hall's *Places Rated Almanac*, which ranked the Hartford metropolitan area 20th for its cultural offerings, out of 343 such areas in the nation and Canada.

Among the offerings in the Arts and Entertainment District is the Wadsworth Atheneum, on Main Street. This impressive castle is America's oldest continuously operated public art museum. For more than 150 years, it has offered residents and visitors to Greater Hartford the opportunity to see an eclectic collection that includes American, European, and 20th-century art.

The beneficiary of recent physical improvements that have made it accessible to the disabled, the Atheneum provides tours in English and Spanish, hosts a summer folk arts festival, and offers a wide range of programs for children. The museum's Amistad Foundation Collection introduces people of all ages to the African-American experience.

The district is also the location of the 2,819-seat Horace Bushnell Memorial Hall, the foremost performing arts center in Connecticut and the cultural focal point of performing arts in Hartford. Situated across the street from the Connecticut State Capitol, the Bushnell was opened in 1930. It presents touring Broadway shows, concerts by visiting orchestras and artists, the Bank of Boston Showcase series, and a wide range of other programs for children and families. Recent season attendance has topped 400,000.

In addition, the Bushnell is the home of the Hartford Symphony Orchestra, the Hartford Ballet Company, and the Connecticut Opera Association. In 1994, the Bushnell underwent a major renovation, enabling it to mount performances of increasingly challenging Broadway plays, such as *Miss Saigon* and *Phantom of the Opera*, the first of these productions to be staged at the Bushnell.

The Hartford Stage Company, on Church Street between Main and Trumbull Streets, has been a Hartford landmark since 1964. One of the nation's finest regional theaters, the Hartford Stage presents an annual six-play season that includes classics, revivals of contemporary plays, and world premieres of new plays.

In addition, the Hartford Stage offers educational programs for children and adults, such as backstage tours for high school students and publications for schools. During the early 1990s, the popular theater underwent a substantial four-year improvement project.

In May 1995, these outstanding arts centers and many others throughout Hartford got a shot in the arm when the city's Arts and Entertainment District became a reality. During a day of entertainment that included such diverse offerings as performances by dance companies, jazz singers, barbershop quartets, and opera troupes, as well as fashion shows and art and history exhibits. at more than 25 different sites, Connect the Dots took shape in the public mind.

Now, the existence of Hartford's Arts and Entertainment District is underscored in local and regional media with the active promotion of a "minifest" on the first Thursday of every month. Visitors to the district can take advantage of a wealth of free entertainment at participating facilities identified by large, colorful storefront dots. The dots, in turn, are connected on user-friendly maps that provide festival information, help visitors find their way around downtown Hartford, and suggest places for parking and dining.

While the primary goal of the Arts and Entertainment District is to connect new people to the fabulous entertainment that already exists here, Connect the Dots is also an economic development

effort. Already the economic impact of Greater Hartford's cultural industry is more than $100 million.

■   ■   ■

Connect the Dots is helping to put Hartford on the map as an entertainment center, but there is more to arts and entertainment in Hartford than the Arts and Entertainment District. Hartford is a city in love with festivals. It throws some big parties every year, and lots of people show up.

First Night Hartford, managed by the Hartford Downtown Council, for instance, enticed 10,000 people downtown when it debuted in 1989. Since then it has enjoyed increasing attendance annually. The popular family-oriented New Year's Eve festival of the arts and the community is alcohol-free and multicultural and now attracts more than 30,000 people who enjoy 10 hours of diverse entertainment at multiple venues all over downtown Hartford for one modest fee. The program traditionally ends with a parade to Bushnell Park, where a throng of revelers welcomes the new year with a midnight fireworks show.

The Taste of Hartford, held in the Main Street Market, attracts more than 150,000 visitors for four days every June. In addition to a culturally diverse range of foods presented by more than 40 area restaurants, the festival features hours of staged entertainment that includes something for every member of the family.

Riverfest, Hartford's celebration of its aquatic heritage, annually draws a large crowd to Bushnell Park, the riverfront, and Constitution Plaza. Kid'rific, Hartford's festival for children produced by the Hartford Downtown Council and Friends of Downtown, attracts 50,000 people every year. Haunted Happenings and Winter Wonderland, two exciting family entertainment events held in the G. Fox Building on Main Street, attracted a total of more than 100,000 visitors during their first year.

*H*orace Bushnell Memorial Hall is home to the Hartford Ballet, shown here in a production of *Coppélia*, and to the Connecticut Opera, shown at the left performing *Faust*.

*M*ark Lamos, artistic director of the Hartford Stage Company, directs actors on the set of *Arms and the Man*.

Willie's standing on Allyn Street in downtown Hartford, blowing a sweet solo on a seriously tarnished trumpet. Bouncing off the Hartford Civic Center's west wall, the notes he's playing swirl upward into the night.

It's hard to tell if anyone on the roof of the Russian Lady can hear him. They probably don't want to. It's Saturday night in the summer, and the roof of the Russian Lady is a little garden sanctuary above it all.

A few dollars and some coins rest on the velvet inside of Willie's open trumpet case. He's not getting rich, but if somebody gives him a buck, he's happy to blow. Besides, the night is young, and he's in the right place.

The heart of Hartford's new Arts and Entertainment District is also the heart of the city's nightlife. It has gotten a shot of adrenaline in recent years with the addition of restaurants and clubs that are drawing big crowds and attracting renewed attention to downtown Hartford.

The Connecticut Coyotes, Hartford's arena football team, are playing a game against Tampa across the street from Willie's corner, and just an hour ago, a take-a-seat-at-the-bar-and-wait crowd packed Coaches, the hot sports bar behind Hartford's historic train station, which shares Union Place with a half dozen other restaurants and night spots.

Walk down Union Place tonight

and you'll see people dining on the patio at Hot Tomatoes, waiting to do some stylin' at Mezzanotte, and rollin' with the bon temps at Bourbon Street North. So many people showed up for the opening of the Brick Yard, a new club just up the street from Coaches, reported *Hartford Courant* columnist Pat Seremet, that four patrons passed out and couldn't fall down.

Up on Trumbull Street, the Bar With No Name doesn't need one to draw a crowd. The Civic Cafe is dishing up culinary innovations. They've got the windows open at Zuzu's, where savvy espresso demons have staked out their favorite sofa on the mezzanine before the predictable throng descends. Just around the corner, at the Blue Star, the band is delivering some smokin' blues. And a short walk from there back toward Union Place, a crowd is scarfing tangy ribs at Black-Eyed Sally's B B Q & Blues, where nationally renowned blues guitarist Lucky Peterson took his music out on Asylum Street during a blistering set the night the club opened.

Willie would have receptive audiences outside plenty of other restaurants and clubs serving up everything from tandoori chicken to tasty zydeco. Whether one seeks food for the stomach or food for the soul, Hartford can oblige.

But Willie decides to stay on Allyn Street. In an hour or so, thousands of people will pour out of the civic center. If the Coyotes win, they may be howling at the moon, and Willie may get a chance to play "Werewolves of London."

Jazz al Fresco

It's a Monday night in July, and maybe, just maybe, the great Dave Brubeck could keep Terry D'Italia home tonight if he showed up at Terry's house and played a private show. Maybe—if Dave provided the refreshments, too.

Tonight is the kickoff of another season of Monday Night Jazz at Bushnell Park, the longest-running major outdoor music festival in Hartford and the longest-running free jazz series in the United States. For five weeks each summer, as a diverse crowd assembles for the concerts, all the possibilities of what community really means blossom in Bushnell Park every Monday night.

But Monday Night Jazz is not Hartford's only jazz festival. In fact, if you like your jazz served al fresco, then you've got a lot to pick from. In addition to Monday Night Jazz, there is the Greater Hartford Festival of Jazz, which annually fills the park for three straight nights at the end of July, and RAW Jazz, the sometimes-funky-sometimes-outré-but-never-uninteresting show mounted in Arbor Street's Day Playground every year by that bastion of the avant-garde, Real Art Ways.

So where else would a respectable jazz devotee like Terry D'Italia, who has been attending Monday Night Jazz for more than a decade, take his family tonight?

Think about it this way:

As dusk starts to fall, the kids down behind the Pumphouse are still enjoying a spirited game of soccer. Mr. Moon, smiling widely, polished to a high luster and puffed up to about the size of a beach ball, has just risen above the low-rise buildings south of the park. The lights of the city skyline are winking on. God's air conditioner is on the "low" setting, blowing out of the south and wafting the mixed aromas of hot dogs and citronella candles across the lawn. The chardonnay is cold, and the band is hot. The grass is green, and Terry D'Italia's toes are in it.

Hey, where's Brubeck?

$\mathcal{T}$he 200-year-old Old State House has recently undergone a $12 million restoration. At right, Wilson "Bill" Faude, the convivial executive director of this historic gathering place.

No matter whom you talk to in the Hartford arts community (and no community in Hartford better exemplifies either the promise of diversity or the healthy exchange of perspectives), there is agreement that reframing Hartford as an arts and entertainment center can succeed only if the undertaking is grounded in celebration of the community.

In that context, no downtown Hartford site more richly deserves to be thought of as the center than the Old State House. Regardless of the direction from which you approach Hartford, all the highway signs are based on the distance to this historic community gathering place. And when visitors to Hartford's revitalized riverfront start climbing the terraced steps to Constitution Plaza in 1997, the first sight to greet them will be the green oasis of this grand building's East Side Park, adorned with new iron fencing and gas lanterns.

It's almost impossible to believe that a scant 20 years ago this building was scheduled for destruction to make room for a parking lot. In the new Hartford, the Old State House couldn't have a more exciting role.

Never more secure in its two centuries of existence, the Old State House is getting a new lease on life. Its $12 million restoration complete, it can become the equivalent of Boston's Faneuil Hall for Hartford—a place for people to gather, to get their bearings, to share ideas, to explore their individual pasts, and to imagine their collective future.

And no matter which way you turn, as you exit its doors, this building most assuredly will be the gateway to Hartford's Arts and Entertainment District.

■   ■   ■

How significant is the Old State House to Hartford? It reeks of this city's heritage.

The square on which it resides was set aside for a communal center by the original colonists nearly 350 years ago. Hartford's first two community meetinghouses were built here. The first settlers to die were interred here.

For two centuries, presidents of the United States, candidates for public office, and other dignitaries have spoken here. General George Washington and Connecticut governor Jonathan Trumbull first met the French armies in America here. In May 1797, Declaration of Independence signatory Oliver Wolcott presided over the first session of the Connecticut State Senate here and accepted the resignation of Oliver Ellsworth as federal senator to become, at Washington's request, the third chief justice of the United States Supreme Court. Charles Dickens visited its courtrooms when he toured America in 1842. President Jimmy Carter came here to announce that the historic nuclear submarine *Nautilus* would return permanently to Connecticut.

But the Old State House's significance is more than merely historical. It is expected to play an increasingly vital role in social discourse.

"This building will be a fun and educational place," says Wilson "Bill" Faude, its executive director. "You won't have to be a scholar to get a kick out of it. There will be concerts, events, places people can rent

for receptions, weddings, and cocktail parties. It's going to be a real meetinghouse—a building that communicates."

The guiding aesthetic in the restoration has been that the public should feel welcome. Below the great east portico, the completely renovated entrance will open upon the building's (and arguably the city's) central hub, where a visitors information center, the Connecticut Historical Society's new 7,000-square-foot Museum of Connecticut History (an addition to the complex built beneath the Main Street courtyard), and the new museum shop will be located. Upstairs, the building's lavishly restored halls will offer permanent and changing displays and space for meetings.

"Part of what makes a city strong is revitalization and jobs," Faude told *CONNSTRUCTION* magazine in 1995. "Here you have this $10 million-plus project. That's jobs. You start with jobs in construction and then you add the tourists who will come to see the Old State House and stay to eat and buy. People who live and work nearby take pride in the area and everyone starts to reinvest."

■   ■   ■

Just a mile up the road, practically spitting distance from downtown, another cornerstone of the dream of making Hartford an entertainment mecca grew like rolling thunder out of the industrial flatlands of the North Meadows in 1995. It's called the Meadows Music Theatre. Nothing has been more eagerly awaited in Hartford in a long time.

Built at a cost of some $30 million, the Meadows Music Theatre is one of America's most unusual concert sites. Constructed on a 19-acre parcel of city land in a part of Hartford distinguished mostly by the array of automobile dealerships, the Meadows is only the second indoor-outdoor amphitheater anywhere. Equipped with a heating system and retractable walls that will enclose its 7,500 seats, it can host events year-round. When the retractable walls are opened, another 23,000 music fans can sit on the high lawn that rises behind the reserved seating.

The Meadows quickly proved itself to be a success. During an inaugural season that ran for only 12 weeks, it racked up a total attendance of 330,000, 40 percent more than projected.

That's not surprising, really. Increasingly, big amphitheaters have become the sites of preference for rock bands. The slate of concerts for the Meadows' first summer series, for instance, often paralleled the shows being offered at Great Woods, the popular amphitheater south of Boston that Connecticut music lovers often traveled to for shows in the past.

Now the Meadows is keeping them home, and no one in Hartford is missing the economic significance of that. In addition to tax revenues, Hartford benefits from a nice chunk of the venue's ticket sales. And immediately, the Meadows created a reported 700 new jobs.

Downtown business leaders, only blocks from this magnet for prospective consumers, greeted the opening of the Meadows enthusiastically. As traditional business travel slows down during summer months, the Meadows routinely attracts thousands of concertgoers, who also are expected to pack Hartford's restaurants and hotels.

But there is more to the story than that. From the crest of the Meadows' steep lawn, you have a spectacular view of the Hartford skyline. As city skylines go, it's an attractive one. If the skyscrapers that went up in the last 20 years did not contribute to a sense of community, they lent a certain authority to a city that too often has perceived itself as in the shadow of New York and Boston. Standing there, at the summit of the Meadows lawn, one can't help but feel that maybe Hartford, no longer willing to be second fiddle to anyone, is finally stepping up to the plate.

$\mathcal{G}$ood music is available everywhere in Hartford—from the new Meadows Music Theatre to the Main Street Market.

ove sports? We've got the bases covered.

In Hartford, the quest for spectator sports starts at the Hartford Civic Center, the region's major sports arena. The civic center is home to the National Hockey League's Hartford Whalers, Connecticut's foremost professional sports team; the Continental Basketball Association's Connecticut Pride; and the Arena Football League's Connecticut Coyotes.

Playing 44 home games each season, the Whalers are Hartford's preeminent downtown evening entertainment attraction. "The Whalers make a tremendous contribution to the vitality of downtown Hartford," says Russ Gregory, the Whalers' senior vice president of marketing and communications.

During the 1990s, as the team's performance has improved, so has attendance at home games. The Greater Hartford Chamber of Commerce and the Hartford Downtown Council are working closely with the Whalers to

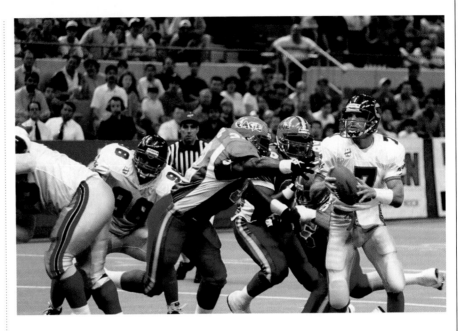

boost interest locally and ensure the team's continued vitality.

Local businessman Brian Foley, who purchased the Connecticut Pride in 1995, saw "a real need to provide affordable family entertainment downtown," says Tyler Jones, a spokesman for the team. Foley's goals are to keep costs down and deliver "a great entertainment package," Jones adds. In addition,

responding to patron requests that he hire local players, Foley drafted University of Connecticut basketball stars Donnie Marshall, Kevin Ollie, and Tate George for his team's debut year.

The civic center is also a home away from home for the consistently dominant University of Connecticut Huskies, whose home court is Gampel Pavilion at the university's Storrs campus. In 1995, Connecticut's women's basketball team became only the second in NCAA history to have an undefeated season.

Baseball aficionados can visit Beehive Field in nearby New Britain, where the class AA Hardware City Rock Cats have the home field advantage. In New Haven, the class AA Ravens are the home team. New Britain also fields a professional soccer team, the United Wolves.

The International Skating Center of Connecticut, in Simsbury, is one of the world's finest ice skating facilities and the home of skating champions Oksana Baiul and Viktor Petrenko. The

complex includes an Olympic rink, an NHL hockey rink, and 2,000 seats.

The PGA tour stops every summer at the Tournament Players Club in nearby Cromwell for the Canon Greater Hartford Open, one of the region's most popular sports events. Top professional golfers compete with each other, as well as with celebrities, in the tournament's pro-am segment.

In addition to all those options, Greater Hartford offers sports fans the annual Pilot Pen International Tennis Tournament at the Connecticut Tennis Center in New Haven, four automobile racing tracks, a greyhound racing track, and big-screen horse racing theaters.

Greater Hartford also presents a wealth of possibilities for those whose athletic tastes run toward more active recreation. Canoeing, swimming, kayaking, and tubing are popular activities on several area rivers and lakes. Motorboating, rowing, and fishing are all on the upswing along the length of the increasingly clean Connecticut River.

If you prefer land activities, Greater Hartford offers plenty to do. From horseback riding to hot-air ballooning, there is something for everyone. There are more than 50 public and private golf courses and 10 ski areas within the region. Connecticut has more than 100 state parks and forests with a variety of outdoor recreational opportunities, including picnicking, camping, hunting, snowmobiling, and ice skating. And 18 state campgrounds offer more than 1,500 sites for campers.

Left: The Arena Football League's Connecticut Coyotes and the National Hockey League's Hartford Whalers are major sports attractions at the Hartford Civic Center. Right: Greg Norman at the Canon Greater Hartford Open.

$\mathcal{R}$esidents of Hartford have endless opportunities to enjoy artistic treasures. They can visit the Wadsworth Atheneum, America's oldest continuously operated public art museum, or Real Art Ways, Hartford's leading alternative arts institution, under the watchful eye of Will Wilkins.

From diverse dining at the popular Taste of Hartford, to exciting night life, to wild and woolly activities for children at Kid'rific, produced by the Hartford Downtown Council and Friends of Downtown, Hartford's Arts and Entertainment District has it all.

CROSSROADS:
HARTFORD'S
MULTICULTURAL
NEIGHBORHOODS

James, Yvonne, and Kendyl Cheek, residents of Hartford's Blue Hills neighborhood.

*J*ust because downtown Hartford offers the entertainment seeker, the diner, and the shopper a treasure chest of opportunities, you shouldn't expect to find an "X" marking "*the* spot" on any map of Greater Hartford. In fact, there are treasures throughout the city. And you don't have to dig too deep into Hartford's neighborhoods to find them.

Picture a day in the not-so-distant future. You've come to Hartford to visit the revitalized riverfront. You'll spend the morning on the river, taking in the activities available in this new aquatic park, including a sightseeing cruise, and visit the tall ship that's permanently docked there.

Late in the morning, you make your way across Constitution Plaza to the Old State House, where you pick up a map of the Arts and Entertainment District and the downtown shopping area. You wander out to Main Street, mulling over far more options than you have time for.

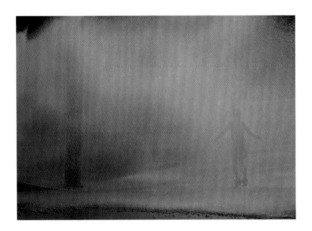

No matter which way you travel, there are a mind-boggling variety of dining and entertainment options in Hartford's culturally diverse neighborhoods. Head south and Main Street splits off into a trio of old South End thoroughfares—Wethersfield Avenue, Maple Avenue, and, most important, Franklin Avenue. For more than a century, the neighborhood embraced by these streets has been the home of Hartford's Little Italy district.

The *Hartford Yellow Pages* lists nearly 40 restaurants in this area. Not all of them serve Italian food, of course, but that's part of the beauty of cultural diversi-ty. Even in a traditional ethnic neighborhood like this, alternative cultures make themselves known.

Head north on Main Street and you'll soon cross over Interstate 84 into the North End and, just beyond, into the Blue Hills neighborhood. The community defined by Main Street and Albany Avenue is the home of many of Hartford's African-Americans, including more than 40,000 West Indians, whose restaurants and shops line extended strips of Albany Avenue.

Stroll down Farmington Avenue or Asylum Avenue in the West End and you'll be amid an eclectic mix of mansions, parks, museums, and small retail shops as you head toward West Hartford and Farmington. Or you might journey along the rainbow artery of Park Street from South Green through the only contiguous strip of stores in New England owned by Hispanics and on through the expanding cultural diversity of Parkville.

All of these neighborhoods benefit from Hartford's extensive network of parks. The city has a total of 25 parks and playgrounds that offer residents and visitors alike a wealth of recreational opportunities. Indeed, visitors to Hartford parks can enjoy a game of golf, take a dip in a freshwater pond, sightsee while enjoying a boat ride, whirl around on an antique carousel, or stroll the nation's oldest municipal rose garden.

As the city approaches the turn of the century, Hartford's Parks and Recreation Department is celebrating the 100th anniversary of the "Reign of Parks," that extraordinary period in history when many of the city's first parks were created. Annual programs in honor of this anniversary include fall and spring bicycle tours and children's festivals in the major parks.

If the measure of cultural diversity is the variety in dining opportunities, then Hartford's neighborhoods get high marks. If you're so inclined, you can munch your way through all of the following cuisines: Afghan, Chinese, German, Indian, Thai, Italian, Cajun, Vietnamese, Japanese, Jamaican, Creole, Korean, Cuban, Mexican, Spanish, Polish, Indian, Mediterranean, Portuguese, and Brazilian. Within walking distance from downtown, you can lunch on anything from hamburgers and fries to deli sandwiches to sushi, red beans,

$\mathcal{A}$ townhouse on Columbia Street in the Frog
Hollow neighborhood.

spring rolls, West Indian beef patties, Portuguese pork, littleneck clams, pizza, pastelillos de carne, arroz con gandules, caldo verde, calamari, boudin, barbecue, or tapas.

■   ■   ■

There's no question cultural diversity is alive in Hartford's neighborhoods, offering the resident and the visitor a wealth of experiences. The soul of that diversity is the neighborhood residents. Their future, and to a large degree the future of Greater Hartford, depends on their collective capacity to preserve and build on what is great and distinctive about their individual heritages. It also depends on the capacity of the region to tap the enormous possibilities Hartford's tapestry of cultures presents.

It will not be easy. As some neighborhoods have thrived, others have been deeply scarred by poverty. Yet, even in those neighborhoods, residents committed to their communities' survival are dreaming great dreams and making extraordinary changes.

In many of the blighted areas, the arts have become almost synonymous with life. Arts centers like the CRT Craftery and the Artists Collective in the North End and Guakia, Inc., on Wethersfield Avenue are communications conduits, important links that tie diverse ethnic traditions to a larger vision of arts that may benefit the city and region as a whole.

■   ■   ■

In Parkville, just beyond the inner ring of downtown Hartford, a neat grid of homes along residential side streets is juxtaposed with broad-shouldered blocks of warehouses. Some of these old factories stand vacant, serving as monuments to the city's industrial past. Others, however, serve as models for a new economy. Indeed, a convergence of arts and business influences is enabling this working-class community to be transformed into a model for surrounding neighborhoods.

Parkville radiates around the intersection where

Sisson Avenue, straight out of Hartford's West End, becomes the industrial and commercial pulse of New Park Avenue as it crosses Park Street headed south. Parkville is a cultural crossroads. This is the traditional home of Hartford's Portuguese residents, many of whom still live here and maintain a strong influence. But more and more, Parkville has also become the home of other ethnic populations—Hispanics and Asians from perhaps a dozen countries.

Parkville is also one of Hartford's many living laboratories, a community where the arts are coming alive in a neighborhood that has been striving to survive and hold on to its heritage. Will Wilkins, the director of Real Art Ways (RAW), believes the survival of alternative arts venues is analogous to the survival of diverse urban cultures. Both thrive because of their essential vibrancy. Both address the most real and unvarnished truths of life. Both struggle to surmount economic barriers. If they are to make it, both must display a rare mixture of sensitivity and toughness.

"This is a community with tremendous potential to work," Wilkins says expansively, as though there are no walls at RAW, as though one exits stage left directly onto Arbor Street. "These are working people with strong family values. Parkville has a lot of heart and a lot of resiliency."

So does RAW. Since 1989, the organization has made its home in what used to be the Underwood Typewriter Company. A big, sprawling building that dominates one side of Arbor Street, it's a model for reclamation of old industrial space.

Not a single theater group or gallery, RAW is an

The language in a brochure about the Artists Collective makes a noble attempt to convey the enormity of the miracle that has happened here for 25 years: "The Artists Collective teaches children how to dance, paint, and make music. How to smile, laugh, and dream. Students learn discipline and a sense of pride, accomplishment, and their own worth. The Artists Collective prepares children for performances, exhibits, and life."

The brochure says famed alto saxophonist Jackie McLean and his wife, Dollie, a dancer and actress, founded the

Artists Collective. What it does not say is that this gift to the children of Greater Hartford was part of a progression of events that resulted from Jackie McLean's addiction to and ultimate redemption from the dark spell of drugs. And it does not say that Dollie, who reports, "I never planned to make this project my life mission," has, nevertheless, been its mother and its engine for a quarter of a century.

The Artists Collective is known nationally for helping young people discover their dreams. The 15,000-plus kids who have been prepared for

performances, exhibits, and life have received these blessings within the walls of an old Catholic church that was built in 1927 and slated to be torn down in 1975. Within blocks of that building where lives are saved quite literally every day, other lives have been lost over matters as trivial as which side of the street is one's "turf."

A Harvard University study called Project Zero identified the Artists Collective as one of five models for urban "safe havens" in the United States. "In economically disadvantaged communities throughout the United States," says the project's report, "safe havens . . . are the artistic creations of dedicated visual and performing artists. For decades, these artist educators have been offering communities of learners—many of them disenfranchised from mainstream institutions—alternative arenas of success and promise."

Every year, in addition to the incalculable service it provides to talented youngsters, the Artists Collective enriches the cultural life of the Hartford community through performances by both students and luminaries in the fields of dance, music, and theater. Ray Charles, Dizzy Gillespie, Roberta Flack, Art Blakey, B. B. King, Billy Taylor, and Wynton Marsalis are just a few of the famous artists who have contributed their talents to this cause.

When the Artists Collective finally moves to a new cultural arts center it will soon build on Albany Avenue, someone should place above the door a sign that says exactly the opposite of the one Dante encountered when he descended into the Inferno.

"THE ARTS HELP TO KEEP COMMUNITIES ALIVE. THEY BRING NEIGHBORS TOGETHER FOR SHARED EXPERIENCES THAT ARE REAFFIRMING, AND THEY ATTRACT VISITORS WHO LEARN SOMETHING NEW ABOUT OTHER PEOPLE."

—WILL WILKINS, DIRECTOR, REAL ART WAYS

organization committed to an artistic mission—offering an alternative to the mainstream. Take in a RAW show and you'll need to pick up your feet as well as waive your preconceptions.

"I believe in a model for arts organizations that reinforces and revitalizes communities," Wilkins says.

In Parkville, Wilkins has found a community that informs RAW's aesthetic. And he's making a major investment in that community. RAW is quadrupling its space, expanding into a multipurpose arts complex that includes a movie/video theater with seating for approximately 140 people, a 200-seat performing arts space, three galleries, a cafe, a community room, and outdoor concert space.

Wilkins hopes RAW will encourage more people to visit Parkville and discover its charms. That hope is not without precedent. In 1993, Spaghetti Warehouse, a restaurant chain, opened a successful restaurant nearby in another former industrial building on Bartholomew Avenue. Popular from the day it opened, to great fanfare, the restaurant serves thousands every week. In 1994, a giant Stop & Shop supermarket opened on New Park Avenue at the site of an old factory destroyed by fire. And the Gotham Lounge, a nightclub that debuted in 1995, has emerged as one of Greater Hartford's premier venues for aficionados of the Latin beat. Dance enthusiasts, who come to hear the hot salsa and merengue bands, pack the club every weekend.

"The arts help to keep communities alive," Wilkins says. "They bring neighbors together for shared experiences that are reaffirming, and they attract visitors who learn something new about other people. And they can encourage people to visit Hartford's neighborhoods and enjoy what they have to offer."

■   ■   ■

RAW is only one example of Hartford arts institutions that are committed to preserving communities and nurturing diverse cultures. The North End, for instance, has the CRT Craftery, the only community-based African-American visual arts gallery that operates year-round in Connecticut and one of the premier African-American galleries in America.

For more than two decades, the Craftery has presented visual arts exhibitions and programming that focus on the contributions and achievements of minority artists and the African-American heritage. "Most of America's African-American galleries are based in New York and Boston," says Jonathon Bruce, the Craftery's director. "It's unusual for a city like Hartford to have a gallery like this."

Bruce sees the Craftery as creating an aesthetic bridge between the North End communities and downtown Hartford. Located at 1445 Main Street, in a building it has occupied for a decade, the Craftery is "on the cusp of downtown, going north into the residential section," he says, a good location for both North End residents and visitors, and it has ample street parking and is accessible by bus.

The Craftery often collaborates on projects with the Wadsworth Atheneum, the Artists Collective, and other arts institutions and with the Hartford Board of Education. But, like Wilkins, Bruce defines his institution as much more than a gallery. "We're not just art on the wall," he says. "The Craftery is about people in the community who make a contribution. Art excites and stimulates, clarifies and confounds, heals and restores.

The beat heats up when the West Indian Festival takes over the Main Street Market.

$\mathcal{N}$ew England's only Hispanic commercial marketplace is a feast for the eyes and ears of this Park Street resident.

$\mathcal{C}$ostumes from many nations add to the colorful fabric of Parkfest.

"GUAKIA SERVES AN IMPOVERISHED NEIGHBORHOOD, BUT THERE IS A GREAT RICHNESS OF SPIRIT HERE AND GREAT JOY!"

—MARCELINA SIERRA, EXECUTIVE DIRECTOR, GUAKIA, INC.

It has the power to transform lives and change minds, if only it can reach them. That's what we've been doing for the past 23 years—bringing the power of art and craft to Greater Hartford's minority communities."

In the South End, Guakia, Inc., performs a similar function for Latino children and families. Founded in 1983, Guakia (Spanish for "we") is a nonprofit organization devoted "to the reaffirmation, enhancement, and preservation of Puerto Rican art, culture, and heritage in Hartford and the Northeast."

Guakia, Inc., sponsors a bilingual school staffed by 12 teachers who help 300 students from diverse cultures and from throughout Greater Hartford learn about both visual and performing arts after school every afternoon and on Saturdays. The school grants more than 60 scholarships every semester.

Since 1993, Guakia, Inc., also has been the home of Connecticut's only theater devoted exclusively to the Puerto Rican experience. Its six annual presentations are warmly received by the community and, says Marcelina Sierra, Guakia's executive director, there is strong community support for the program.

"Artists love to perform at the theater," she says. "It is intimate and close to the community. Whenever we put on a production, you could cut the energy with scissors. Guakia serves an impoverished neighborhood, but there is a great richness of spirit here and great joy!"

■   ■   ■

Arts organizations like these are only one example of the kinds of groups that are involved in reforming and restoring Hartford's neighborhoods.

Throughout the city, citizens groups are investing time, energy, and creativity to make Hartford's neighborhoods better and more livable. Hartford Areas Rally Together (HART), for instance, has been committed to improving Hartford neighborhoods for 20 years, earning it the distinction of being the oldest organization of its type in New England.

HART serves neighborhoods in Hartford's South and West Ends. An umbrella organization, it provides support for more than 45 different groups, ranging from neighborhood associations to school groups to block clubs. The range of community improvement activities it supports is equally diverse, including programs in crime prevention, housing, education, and jobs and economic development.

All of these programs benefit tremendously from the involvement of Hartford volunteers. Nearly 400 parents, for instance, volunteer each year for an after-school program supported by HART. The program, which encompasses 16 schools citywide, provides opportunities for more than 3,000 youngsters to get tutoring assistance and help with homework, to learn how to use computers, and to participate in recreational programs.

More than 5,000 people participate in at least one HART-supported activity each year, and that involvement is the greatest strength of the organization, says Jim Boucher, HART's director. "Citizen involvement is the most exciting part of what we do," says Boucher. "When citizens become leaders and take an active role in making their neighborhoods better, exciting things happen and everyone benefits."

The dynamic interplay between arts and community groups is also central to the work of the Charter Oak Cultural Center.

Left: Parkville youngsters enjoy the Art in the Park program sponsored by Real Art Ways.

Owner Dolores Sullivan serves up a tasty treat at Lena's, her restaurant on Park Street.

Scattered throughout the city's neighborhoods, parks provide breathing space for Hartford youngsters.

Housed in the historic Beth Israel Temple, which was constructed in 1876 as the spiritual home of Hartford's first Jewish community, the cultural center may be the greatest symbol of freedom of expression in Hartford. The temple was built only after its congregants and other Connecticut Jews petitioned the Connecticut State Assembly for the right to worship in public.

No Hartford arts institution better exemplifies the hope for a united community grounded in open expression and the celebration of many great traditions, and Charter Oak Cultural Center is certainly well positioned for that role. While it is part of Hartford's Arts and Entertainment District, it is physically much closer to one of Hartford's most socially complex neighborhoods than to most of the downtown arts venues.

The center's location seems to reflect its philosophy—its dedication to promoting, exploring, and celebrating diverse cultures, particularly those most strongly represented in Hartford. Recently, for instance, the center's calendar of events included a festival of performances and symposia on Yiddish culture; an evening of dance and music demonstrating the parallels and distinctions between French-speaking communities; a festival in collaboration with the Artists Collective to celebrate the cultural heritage of the people of the African diaspora; concerts of Eastern music and dance; a gospel festival; a literary conference on the topic of Puerto Rican cultural affirmation; a showcase of European Baroque-era music and instruments; and a public forum to announce a 10-year community project with the Connecticut Historical Society to document the story of Hartford's African-Americans between 1734 and 1960.

An impressive effort to celebrate diversity? Sure! But as Anthony Keller, the center's executive director, is quick to underscore, the center has another important role—to serve as a forum for mediation between the various cultural groups in the city and the region. The center's most apparent application of that role is in strengthening its immediate neighborhood, another of those living laboratories in Hartford where the community is experimenting with and learning how to support and benefit from its cultural diversity.

One of Hartford's most diverse neighborhoods, the area surrounding the Charter Oak Cultural Center includes the South Green area of Main Street, with its mix of retail and commercial buildings and restaurants; the racially diverse neighborhood immediately behind the center; Colt Park and the Colt Armory, around which visions and rumors of economic revival constantly swirl; the southern extremity of the Riverfront Recapture project; revitalized historic buildings along Columbus Avenue; and the suffocating poverty of the Dutch Point Housing Project.

No day passes when Tony Keller, a fundamentally optimistic man, does not look at that urban pastiche and see boundless possibilities for collaboration between community groups to preserve and build upon Hartford's many rich cultural traditions. The center is already building bridges between the center and the area's residents, local schools, and community-based institutions.

"For any city to grow and prosper, there must be economic growth," he says, "but cities do not survive on economic solutions alone. There are also human issues, diverse cultures, and neighborhoods. They must be supported and celebrated. They are what make a city great. And the issues raised in defining how to preserve and build upon cultural diversity go right to the root of any city's capacity to endure."

"What is this?" the man inquires. He's holding a big green tropical fruit bristling with horns. The man is an Anglo and clearly not accustomed to finding the fruit in his neighborhood supermarket.

"That's a guanabana," explains Maria Arroyo, smiling. "It's kind of like a mango."

"How do you eat it?" the man asks.

"There are black seeds inside," says Maria. "You have to remove them. Then you can eat the pulp, or you can process it in a blender and make a drink."

"I'll take one," the man says.

On the corner of Park Street and Hungerford Avenue, Maria and her brother Edwin have set up a sidewalk stand in front of La Placita del Pueblo, their father's store. It's early afternoon,

and already they are doing a brisk trade in guanabanas, plantains, and mamays.

On practically any day of the week, this strip of Park Street would be buzzing with people and salsa music. Today there are more people than usual—about 100,000 more.

Today is Parkfest, the annual fair that salutes Greater Hartford's Hispanic community and the street that is its economic and spiritual center. Over the past few years, the scope of the festival has expanded to promote the importance of Park Street not only in Hartford but throughout the region.

"This street is the only Hispanic commercial marketplace in New England," explains Pedro de Pedro, former executive director of the Spanish American Merchants Association. "People come from New York, Rhode Island, and Massachusetts to shop in these stores."

A lot of those repeat customers are expected today. Already the street is choked with people. And the ever-present salsa music that spills out of doorways is competing with a dizzying array of musicians, from small Colombian bands to Peruvian flutists to frenetic dancers. The party stretches all the way from Washington Street to Pope Park, where a children's festival is in full swing.

"This is a celebration of our many cultures," says Pedro, explaining the event's theme, *Bajo el mismo sol* ("Under the same sun"). "Many people think of Hispanics as one culture, but 16 countries are represented here today. There are black people, white people, Indian people.

"There is great loyalty to Park Street. Coming to Parkfest is like coming home."

WHERE HARMONY GROWS

One evening in June, James Riley and six other Jamaicans are tending plots in one of the Knox Parks Foundation's 16 community gardens serving the Greater Hartford area. More than 20 gardeners, all residents of the area, grow vegetables, fruits, and flowers on the two-acre parcel of rich soil behind the Unitarian Meeting House off Bloomfield Avenue.

The gardeners are a diverse lot. "We have people here from Jamaica, Laos, Puerto Rico, Peru, and Eastern Europe," says Riley, who has been growing his own food here every summer for six years. Other farmers have been here even longer.

It is hard to believe that this oasis, surrounded by a buffer of trees, is a scant half mile from the gritty bustle of the Upper Albany District. And from the stately mansions of Prospect Avenue, for that matter.

The gardens are only one of the projects maintained by the Knox Foundation, the mission of which is "to build upon the richness of human and natural resources to make the Hartford area more livable, vibrant, and humane." Created with a trust fund established by former Hartford councilwoman Betty Knox, the foundation also manages a nationally acclaimed school program that makes a GROW LAB available to every school in Hartford and 16 surrounding towns; a year-round series of programs on gardening and crafts for the general public; and a lending library of books, periodicals, and videos.

High school students from throughout the region earn a paycheck and perform valuable community service work while learning about landscaping, grounds care, and gardening as part of the Parks Ranger Program, sponsored by the foundation. And hundreds of adults and children enjoy a weekly story hour in Elizabeth Park, on the border of Hartford and West Hartford, every summer.

It is, perhaps, from the community gardens, seeded throughout Hartford's neighborhoods, that most people know the foundation. People from nearly every ethnic group in Hartford participate in the 20-year-old program. And among the most important things that grow in their gardens are harmony and peaceful coexistence.

*I*n some Hartford neighborhoods, traditional scenes like these are still part of the everyday landscape.

*H*artford's festivals give people an opportunity to explore the ordinary and the extraordinary.

A DIVERSE ECONOMY:
*B*USINESS IN GREATER HARTFORD

*G*iselle Ciarcia, shown with her mother and grandmother, owns the Ciarcia Bakery, founded by her father 30 years ago on Franklin Avenue in Hartford's South End.

orporations positioning themselves to compete in an increasingly global and multicultural world have discovered that survival requires making space for the kinds of diverse ideas that allow businesses to remain flexible, to address the needs of multiple publics, and to grow.

Start exploring Greater Hartford's business sector these days and you will soon find that there are exciting ideas, proposals, and developments at every level—from Hartford's neighborhoods to the overall region. For starters, the regional economy is resilient, thanks to the variety of business and industry. The directory of the Greater Hartford Chamber of Commerce lists a remarkable range of major employers with at least 1,000 employees. These include companies in insurance, retail, health care, banking and finance, education, aerospace, manufacturing, chemicals, food and beverage, and transportation.

Even though Greater Hartford's economy, like that of the entire Northeast, was hit hard by the recession of the late 1980s, Connecticut still has the highest income level in America. In fact, the average per capita income of Greater Hartford is nearly $19,000, 33 percent higher than the national average. And the median household income tops $54,000.

Several factors contribute to Greater Hartford's strong business sector. Regional businesses and their employees benefit from excellent transportation and distribution systems. The region has abundant, affordable utilities. A wide range of progressive banking and financial institutions offer the capital support

businesses need to stay healthy. And, thanks to the public schools, which invest an average of $6,891 in each student every year, and the region's numerous top-rated universities and two- and four-year colleges, Greater Hartford businesses have access to a well-educated and plentiful workforce.

■   ■   ■

Any look at the businesses of Greater Hartford must surely start with the insurance industry. Hartford has long enjoyed a reputation as the "Insurance Capital of the World." Seven of the nation's largest insurance firms—Aetna Life & Casualty, the Travelers Insurance Companies, Connecticut Mutual Life Insurance Company, ITT Hartford Insurance, CIGNA Corporation, Phoenix Home Life Mutual Insurance Company, and Metra Health—are headquartered here. Nearly 80,000 people in Greater Hartford are employed by the insurance, finance, and real estate industries.

Almost 100,000 more people are employed in manufacturing. The region's manufacturing sector includes many Fortune 500 corporations and large multinational organizations. Among the best known are the Barnes Group, United Technologies Corporation (including its divisions Hamilton Standard and Pratt & Whitney and its subsidiary Otis Elevator), the Stanley Works, and Loctite.

Together, the insurance and manufacturing industries make up Greater Hartford's traditional economic base. These industries offer not only diversity but the stability needed to build the economy of the future.

The City of Hartford and the administration of Mayor Mike Peters have played a strong role in keeping businesses in Hartford and attracting new businesses. In 1995, Advest, which had considered relocating, decided to remain in the city. Heublein announced it was moving its corporate headquarters downtown. And Trans-General Life Insurance Company moved to Hartford from outside the area.

Prominent among the region's emerging industries are health care and high technology. Greater

$\mathcal{S}$tanley Works in
New Britain is one
of the many Fortune
500 corporations and
large multinational
organizations in the
Greater Hartford area.

$\mathcal{A}$ worker at Kaman
Aerospace Corporation
in Bloomfield performs
tests on the company's
newest helicopter.

Hartford is served by several nationally distinguished hospitals and health centers, and the rapidly growing health-care industry employs nearly 60,000 people. High tech is expected to be a growth area in the future, thanks to cooperation and increasingly interesting collaboration between the health-care sector, area colleges and universities, the government, and private companies.

In addition to large businesses, Greater Hartford is blessed with successful small to midsized companies. "These businesses are the backbone of the region's economy," says Timothy J. Moynihan, president of the Greater Hartford Chamber of Commerce, "and the outlook for their success is boosted by an aggressive program of business incubators, economic incentives, and financial assistance packages made available through federal, state, and local government and area educational facilities." Moynihan points, for instance, to the fact that several towns in the region have created enterprise zones that offer smaller businesses development and employment incentives and federal tax credits. Further, more than $1 billion is being added to the region's economy through the construction projects that are building the infrastructure for the future.

■   ■   ■

The directory of the Greater Hartford Chamber lists no fewer than 40 regional organizations and agencies devoted to business development. They include federal, state, and local business assistance agencies; education and training programs; sources of financial assistance; international trade organizations; minority enterprise resource centers; research centers; site location and facility planning services; and research and development/technical assistance facilities.

Prominent among these is the Connecticut Capitol Region Growth Council, a private nonprofit corporation committed to enhancing economic development in Hartford and 28 surrounding towns. The Growth Council was established in 1992 by business and government leaders and supports initiatives aimed both at recruiting new businesses and retaining and strengthening the businesses already based here.

One of the council's most significant achievements has been the development of METROFUND, an economic assistance program that is the first of its kind in Connecticut. METROFUND supports both the expansion of existing businesses and the relocation of new businesses to municipalities. Municipalities are required to match METROFUND contributions in varying amounts.

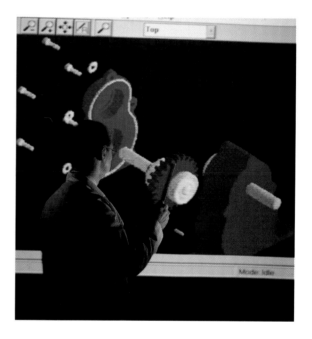

METROFUND's site-readiness component is designed to support businesses involved in projects such as road improvement and the construction of water or sewer lines. The size of the grants is based on the number of categories of new jobs to be created, as well as the amount of the private sector investment.

A revolving loan fund aims to assist capital region firms that may have limited ability to secure loans from existing commercial funding sources or to complete financing packages that require monies in excess of available commercial and equity financing. The loans can be used to cover such expansion-related items as the acquisition of land and buildings, the purchase of machinery and equipment, leasehold improvements, and inventory.

*A*bove right: Training is an ongoing process at Loctite's new research and development facility in Rocky Hill.

In METROFUND's first four months, the Growth Council funded 17 projects with a total of $714,600 in 10 different Greater Hartford communities. Collectively, these projects promised to generate $31.3 million in new capital investment and to create upward of 500 new jobs within the first year.

Those results, says P. Anthony Giorgio, Ph.D., the president and chief executive officer of the Growth Council, are precisely what the council's constituents are looking for. "Community leaders and taxpayers want a regional organization like this that can help to create jobs and build the economy," he says. "Corporations feel the same way. They're willing to support the work we're doing, but they want to see that we're doing something to improve the economy and help Connecticut businesses grow."

Toward that end, Giorgio launched a business visitation program designed to ensure that representatives of the council consistently meet with managers of the region's businesses to provide them with information on how the council can help them meet their needs. The program also enables the council to track these businesses' growth, sales, and expansion activities.

"A majority of companies we've surveyed indicate they expect to expand in the near future," says Giorgio. "Armed with information about their plans and their concerns, we're in a position to work for solutions that benefit many companies and the overall Greater Hartford business climate."

One of the most effective resources available to help the council accomplish this goal is the Connecticut Capitol Region Partnership (CCRP), a collaboration of independent regional organizations spearheaded by the Greater Hartford Chamber of Commerce. Formed in 1995, CCRP provides a formal forum in which member organizations can meet to share resources, with the goal of enhancing the overall quality of life in the region.

CCRP had been in existence for only a short time when the senior managers of one of the companies Giorgio was visiting told him his company was considering purchasing a smaller company and relocating it. Connecticut, they told him, was in competition with another state. Having access to the workforce they would need in the future was imperative, the managers said. Thanks to his organization's involvement in CCRP, Giorgio was able to quickly set up a meeting for the company's managers with leaders of the Capital Region Workforce Development Board and the Capitol Region Education Council.

The Capitol Region Partnership is only one such business development activity sponsored by or supported by the Greater Hartford Chamber of Commerce, which celebrates its 200th anniversary in 1999. "The Chamber also functions as the hub of a network of regional chambers of commerce," says Thomas Groark, chairman of the board of the Chamber. "It provides services to participating chambers and helps them network, share ideas, and have input on the development of the business mix from which the entire region benefits.

"Facilitating networking is one of the Chamber's key functions. The organization holds multiple meetings

From flowers to food, merchants in the Main Street Market do a brisk trade daily.

each year, including monthly meetings, new member receptions, conferences, and seminars that enable members of both the Greater Hartford Chamber and area chambers to get together and share ideas."

■ ■ ■

Business development is a passion throughout Greater Hartford, taking place at the regional level, at the municipal level, and, increasingly, at the neighborhood level. From the North End of Hartford to downtown to the South End, neighborhood business organizations are taking a hard look at the unique strengths of the businesses they represent and outlining development plans for the future.

In downtown Hartford, projects aimed at attracting new businesses, retaining existing businesses, and ensuring that the retail core remains vibrant benefit from the efforts of three important organizations—the Hartford Downtown Council, Business for Downtown Hartford, and the Hartford Marketing Collaborative.

The Hartford Downtown Council is the "downtown branch" of the Greater Hartford Chamber of Commerce. It was formed by the business community in 1974 as a promotional agency and has evolved into a downtown management organization with the mission of making Hartford the economic, cultural, and educational center of the region.

The Downtown Council is funded by the business community to promote businesses and assist in downtown development. "The council supports a wide range of activities," says Anthony M. Caruso, executive director. "They include fostering a safe, clean and attractive city; marketing and promoting the attractions of Hartford; ensuring that the Hartford Whalers remain vital to the community; advancing economic development activities in the city; reaching out to community organizations to leverage their effectiveness; and providing ongoing events and activities for Hartford."

The Downtown Council organizes and promotes special events, including First Night Hartford, the

holiday Festival of Light on Constitution Plaza, and Kid'rific; supplements city maintenance and security programs; and collaborates with other organizations and city agencies concerning marketing, transportation, parking, and other needs of downtown workers and shoppers. "This city thrives on people," says Caruso. "It is key to our survival."

The Hartford Marketing Collaborative was formed in 1993 by the Hartford Downtown Council to promote Hartford activities and attractions. The more than 100 groups, businesses, and individuals that are members of the Marketing Collaborative work together to share ideas and cooperate on efforts to communicate effectively about what is going on in Hartford.

Among the successes of the Marketing Collaborative is the development of MegaWeekend programs. Several times a year, the organization sponsors a weekend of exciting events and entertainment downtown. Popular from the outset, the programs have grown in scope through collaboration with the Hartford Arts Council, sponsor of the monthly First Thursday programs. The MegaWeekend programs always attract large crowds to the downtown core.

Business for Downtown Hartford is an organization of downtown businesses that has more than 150 members. Like the Downtown Council, Business for Downtown Hartford is committed to finding ways to keep downtown Hartford vibrant.

With the Hartford Downtown Council, the organization was instrumental in founding the Hartford

Left: The Ancient Burial Ground, Hartford's oldest cemetery, nestles at the feet of the Gold Building, which houses the world headquarters of United Technologies Corporation.

Guides, who help visitors find their way around downtown, as well as provide information about events, shopping, and attractions; in the passage of an ordinance prohibiting aggressive panhandlers; and in the development of downtown Hartford's Park, Shop and Dine program, which enables shoppers to park for free if they get their parking lot tickets validated by participating merchants. Business for Downtown Hartford also supports members by offering programs that enable small companies to purchase radio advertising together.

Throughout the rest of the city, other business organizations are successfully promoting and developing Hartford's neighborhoods. The Upper Albany Merchants Association, for instance, was formed in the 1980s to assist in the promotion of the largest commercial area in North Hartford. "Since then, we've made great strides in building a strong, representative organization," says Keith Carr, head of the association. "Our objectives are to organize a strong communications network and effective promotional activities to increase utilization of area businesses."

In "Neighborhood of Choice," for instance, a report to the community, the Upper Albany Neighborhood

Collaborative's Economic Development Committee, in which the merchants association is actively involved, outlined the findings of a year-long study of the North End community. The report identified neighborhood assets that could be developed more effectively, such as the rich blend of cultural groups and the large, turn-of-the-century homes. The report also outlined community concerns and specific issues that need to be addressed for economic development to take place in the neighborhood.

Similar work is going on for Park Street. A comprehensive study, outlined in a plan called the "Park Street Revitalization Program," says, "Park Street, a center of Puerto Rican businesses, is a magnet for the city's Latino community, and is one of the most vital retail shopping streets in Hartford." The study outlines a marketplace that is projected to be expanded significantly in the future and defines a clear plan of action for that growth.

In the South End, the Franklin Avenue and South End Merchants Association has an equally comprehensive plan for the ongoing development and revitalization of Hartford's century-old "Little Italy" community. The ambitious plan includes not only developing the neighborhood's businesses but improving the area's housing, employment situation, and social services as well.

At one level or another, most of the best minds in the region are wrestling with the question of how to develop the economy Greater Hartford deserves as it moves into the 21st century. The answer, they are discovering, depends on the capacity of the people of Greater Hartford to work collectively and capitalize on their unique mix of businesses, cultures, and resources.

Nearly all the time, business leaders are discovering, demonstrating an appreciation of diversity and pursuing a cooperative approach to business development produce meaningful results. And that is something worth celebrating.

The headquarters of Aetna Life and Casualty and ITT Hartford, two of America's largest insurance companies.

*H*artford Square North, home of the world headquarters of the Loctite Corporation.

*H*igh-rise office space intersects with diverse options in dining and shopping in State House Square.

*P*hoenix Home Life's distinctive "boat" building on Constitution Plaza, with the Travelers Tower in the background.

*L*eft: The new headquarters of Heublein, Inc., as seen from Constitution Plaza.

*A*bove: The Hartford Civic Center is home to the NHL's Hartford Whalers.
The Civic Center Mall has been a downtown shopping oasis for more than
20 years. Right: Downtown workers on lunch break are reflected in the
Gold Building's mirrorlike facade.

A Healthy Tomorrow:
Health and Education in Greater Hartford

Trinity College junior Lyly Hin in one of the college's many gothic passageways.

*I*f ideas were produce, Greater Hartford would look like a bazaar these days. The region is bursting with products, plans, possibilities.

The shapes, tastes, and smells of this market are more than the sum of the individual components. Everything is bigger than it seems on the surface.

Here, synergy is a commodity. And you can get a lot of it for your money.

In every respect, Greater Hartford is discovering, with growing excitement, that it has both great resilience and great potential. It is a place in thrall with the bold notion of what it is about to become. And two areas of the economy that are becoming stronger are education and health care.

■ ■ ■

From its public school systems to its colleges and universities, Greater Hartford places great importance on education. It is critical to this region's future.

No single segment of the area's economy may better exemplify the power of synergy. Where higher education merges with business and the health-care industry, you get glimpses of a bright economic light that promises to get even brighter tomorrow.

In 1995, the Connecticut General Assembly approved a strategic plan, based on a public-private partnership, to rebuild the University of Connecticut. Called UConn 2000, the plan calls for an investment of more than $1.75 billion to be made over a 10-year period to rebuild the university's main campus in Storrs, east of Hartford, as well as to construct and equip academic and research facilities in Storrs and at other regional campuses.

The long-term impact could be even more significant, however. Studies conducted by the Connecticut Center for Economic Analysis indicate that in addition to improving the state's leading public university, UConn 2000 could result in nearly 13,000 jobs being added to the state's economy during the first years of the coming century. The studies also project that Connecticut's real gross state product, a measure of the total economic activity of the state, will increase by more than $2.6 billion because of the initiative. And the studies did not even consider the economic activity that could occur because of the increase in out-of-state enrollment at the university, the increases in private and federal grants to the university, the increases in joint university-industry projects, and the increases in private funds to the university.

■ ■ ■

Other colleges and universities in Greater Hartford are making equally profound progress.

Trinity College, founded in 1832, is one of the oldest independent liberal arts colleges in the country. It offers 750 courses in 35 majors.

Trinity calls itself "the college in the city." That identity reflects not only the physical location of Trinity's campus in Hartford's South End but also the college's commitment to addressing the challenges and building upon the opportunities inherent in Hartford's complex urban environment.

Trinity, says President Evan Dobelle, is engaged in a "conversation" about cities in general and with the city of Hartford in particular. That dialogue concerns the role of academic institutions in solving urban problems and shaping tomorrow's urban environments. Aided by a substantial grant from the Pew Charitable Trusts, the college has positioned itself for a prominent role in Hartford's future by developing an ambitious project called the Urban Curricular Initiative.

"WE NEED HARTFORD AND IT NEEDS US. WE'RE DEDICATED TO SERVING THE LEARNING NEEDS OF PROFESSIONALS, . . . BUT WE'RE ALSO DEDICATED TO SUPPORTING AND STRENGTHENING THE COMMUNITY."

—ANN STUART, PRESIDENT, HARTFORD GRADUATE CENTER

The project includes designing and implementing a program that will examine cities in a wide range of historical and cultural contexts, from the perspectives of the humanities and the social sciences. It will result in new courses to ensure undergraduates ample opportunities to make the study of cities an important part of their education. It will support forums to explore urban issues. And it will expand the involvement of Hartford-based professionals in various capacities.

Trinity has already been awarded a major grant from the federal Department of Housing and Urban Development to establish the Community Outreach Partnership Center Program. Its purpose is to analyze neighborhood challenges and develop strategies for revitalization.

■ ■ ■

The University of Hartford, with its 320-acre campus in West Hartford, is on the cusp of Bloomfield and Hartford's North End. Founded in 1877, it offers educational and career programs in 91 undergraduate and 74 graduate majors in nine schools and colleges.

The university is actively committed to developing educational programs that prepare students for employment in Greater Hartford. For instance, the university's Barney School of Business and Public

Administration launched an actuarial studies program in the late 1980s to prepare students for a career that is likely to continue to experience strong growth.

The university also has programs in occupational therapy and physical therapy, both fast-growing health professions. The university's College of Education, Nursing and Health Professions provides students with the education required to enter a wide range of service-oriented careers. In addition to nursing, students can earn degrees in medical technology, respiratory therapy, health science, and radiologic technology. The college offers predental, preoptometric, prechiropractic, and pre-physical therapy programs as well.

■ ■ ■

Through its innovative programs, the University of Hartford continues to play a strong role in shaping the region and serving its diverse needs. The new Business and Industry Resource Initiative (BIRI), for instance, aims to make the university's resources more available to the region's corporate community. While targeting corporate clients in Greater Hartford, BIRI has also established relationships with foreign firms and trade organizations to help them develop business opportunities regionally.

The university's Downtown Center, at 99 Pratt Street, is both a place of learning and evidence of the university's commitment to the revitalization of Hartford. The center offers downtown employees the opportunity to take more than 50 undergraduate, graduate, and noncredit courses in such areas as management, insurance, marketing, and computer science.

■ ■ ■

Affiliated with Rensselaer Polytechnic Institute, the Hartford Graduate Center was created in 1955, when United Aircraft, a forerunner of United Technologies,

*E*ducation is an important facet of life in Hartford. Trinity College (top) and St. Joseph College are only two of the four-year, two-year, and technical colleges in the area.

$\mathcal{T}$he West Hartford campus of the University of Connecticut offers students a wide range of programs that prepare them for employment in Greater Hartford, including actuarial studies and nursing, medical technology, respiratory therapy, health science, and radiologic technology.

was looking for creative ways to keep engineers on the cutting edge of their profession without having to send them to remote locations for further education. Originally housed in East Hartford, the school built a plant in downtown Hartford in 1970.

The mission of the Graduate Center is to meet the lifelong learning needs of professionals. While still addressing the needs of engineers, the population it was founded to serve, the school has expanded its programs significantly over the years.

Like other area universities, the Graduate Center is planning for growth in the region's health-care industry. Today, the Graduate Center's School of Management offers graduate degree programs in health-care administration.

"We need Hartford and it needs us," says Ann Stuart, president of the Graduate Center. "Our aim is to help professionals stay on the cutting edge of their disciplines today. We're dedicated to serving the learning needs of professionals now and in the coming century, but we're also dedicated to supporting and strengthening the community. A high percentage of our alumni return to Connecticut industry to strengthen it and keep it competitive."

■   ■   ■

St. Joseph College, in West Hartford, was founded more than 60 years ago by the Sisters of Mercy. Today, it is devoted to improving the quality of life for its women students and the community.

The college's innovative "Saturday Academy" program, supported by a grant from Aetna Life & Casualty, aims to stem school dropout rates among inner-city youngsters. Each semester a class of Hartford middle school students nominated by guidance counselors and teachers attend Saturday classes at the college. The youngsters get the kind of help with core subjects such as mathematics, writing and reading, and science that can make the difference between dropping out of school, and society, and going on for advanced education.

The college is equally devoted to providing women

with the education they need to embark upon virtually limitless career options. The academic offerings are constantly being refined to help students prepare for the jobs of the future. The college's academic tracks include programs in the sciences, dietetics and family studies, nursing, business administration, and mathematics and computer science.

■   ■   ■

It is in the interaction between Hartford's educational institutions and the region's health-care industry that one sees what can happen when there is synergy.

When Connecticut Children's Medical Center was being constructed on the campus of Hartford Hospital, for instance, among the groups that welcomed the idea of the center was the Southside Institutions Neighborhood Alliance (SINA). SINA is a collaboration of Hartford Hospital, Trinity College, and the Institute of Living, a not-for-profit, comprehensive center for the evaluation, treatment, and follow-up care of people with psychiatric, emotional, and addictive disorders.

SINA began its 1994 annual report by saying, "The Connecticut Children's Medical Center holds the promise of providing multiple benefits for the area; because its character is solely devoted to children, it is committed to making primary care and outreach services readily available for them throughout the city."

Citing the significant economic impact the medical center would have on Hartford, the report pointed out that it would create jobs for the equivalent of 713 full-time employees and generate an annual payroll of nearly $30 million. Further, the report noted, "The future potential for spin-off from biomedical companies and additional physician offices in the area will enhance Hartford's resources and help stimulate future economic growth."

The Children's Medical Center is only one example of several health-care facilities in Greater Hartford that are preparing for the future. Hartford Hospital, on whose campus the medical center is being built, has been a Hartford fixture for 137 years.

With more than 800 beds, this regional general and surgical care facility offers specialties in cancer, trauma, pediatrics, transplants, and cardiology. Equipped with a helicopter service for patients requiring critical care, Hartford Hospital is the premier specialty referral hospital in north-central Connecticut. Across town from the Hartford Hospital/Children's Medical Center complex, the Saint Francis/Mount Sinai Health Care System has also been buzzing with activity.

In 1990, Saint Francis Hospital, founded by the Sisters of St. Joseph of Chambery, affiliated with Mount Sinai Hospital, which had been created by Jewish physicians. The affiliation created an institution whose specialties include nearly every major area of medicine.

Since the affiliation, the new health-care system has been engaged in ongoing enhancement of its facilities and technology. In 1993, the hospitals opened the Saint Francis/Mount Sinai Regional Cancer Center. Hartford's first medical rehabilitation center opened on the Mount Sinai campus in 1995. And the latest addition to the complex is a 10-story facility that will have rooms for outpatient surgery and critical care patients, as well as a pavilion for women's health.

Hartford Hospital, the Connecticut Children's Medical Center, and the Saint Francis/Mount Sinai System are linked through their affiliation with the University of Connecticut Health Center, and each of the hospitals is a teaching facility for the UConn School of Medicine. A major component of the health center's strategic plan is the development of an urban health network that will work with the health-care institutions already affiliated with the health center to provide primary care for medically underserved children and adults in Hartford and to coordinate programs addressing addiction, AIDS, and poisoning in the home, the workplace, and the environment.

While the health center's strategic plan clearly embraces the idea of collaborating with Greater Hartford hospitals to ensure the highest quality of health care for the citizens of the region, the center is focusing increasingly on the important role of health research.

Biomedical research is "the field from which the most dramatic and beneficial medical discoveries are likely to come, and this is the field on which the Strategic Plan quite deliberately has focused," says a report on the health center. In fact, the birth of one Connecticut biotechnology company, TargeTech, of Meriden, was the direct consequence of research by two members of the health center faculty.

There are reasons to expect more such developments. Health care, as the Greater Hartford Chamber has noted in its overview of the regional economy, is projected to be a major regional growth area in the years to come. As the region's educational institutions continue to gear up for the future, collaborations between them and health-care institutions will undoubtedly result in more jobs and a stronger local economy.

Such collaborations will also mean that the residents of Greater Hartford will have access to both top-quality education and excellent health care. In fact, no one who lives in the region is out of reach of either amenity.

Those seeking an education can pick from many community colleges and more than 30 independent trade and occupational schools, as well as from Greater Hartford's 12 major colleges and universities.

Every resident of Greater Hartford is also within easy reach of a highly qualified general medical and surgical hospital. There are more than a dozen hospitals in the area, with a total of more than 2,700 beds. In addition, the region's health-care providers include specialized hospitals, walk-in medical and dental clinics, optical service centers, retirement and assisted living centers, and nursing homes.

Overall, the health of the region is good—and getting better every day.

Connecticut Children's Medical Center, on the campus of Hartford
Hospital, is the newest addition to an already long list of medical facilities
in the Greater Hartford area.

𝒜 Hartford fixture for more than 135 years, Hartford Hospital offers specialties in cancer, trauma, pediatrics, transplants, and cardiology. Saint Francis Hospital (top), now part of the Saint Francis/Mount Sinai Health Care System, and the University of Connecticut Health Center are among the other premier medical facilities in the area.

$\mathcal{L}$acrosse is becoming a popular sport among high school students like these at Hartford Public High School.

$\mathcal{A}$ May Day celebration brings schoolchildren together at Hartford's Noah Webster School.

Graduation is
a time for hugs
and smiles at
Hall High School
in West Hartford.

Weaver High School
is one of several high
schools in the
Hartford area that
offers an honors
program in physics.

Hartford:

PROUD, BEAUTIFUL, AND SAFE

*O*fficer Kelly Gerent, at the police department's stable on Vine Street, is the only woman on mounted police patrol in Hartford.

teve Campo might have penned the words "If you build it, they will come." He is certainly a beneficiary of that philosophy. For the past few years, subscriptions to TheaterWorks, the downtown Hartford theater of which he is executive director, have been increasing annually.

Campo attributes this success in part to the fact that more and more people are discovering (or rediscovering) Hartford and what it has to offer. "We're doing good theater," he says. "If you do something well enough, long enough, word gets around."

Everywhere you look, there are more and more people in downtown Hartford. Consider:

- As a result of a Greater Hartford Convention and Visitors Bureau campaign called "Bring It Home to Hartford" and significant upgrading of downtown hotels, occupancy rates have been climbing significantly. Every year, nearly 350 conventions attract more than 137,000 people to downtown Hartford, where they spend an estimated $80.5 million.
- The six biggest downtown arts and entertainment attractions (the Bushnell, the Wadsworth Atheneum, the Connecticut Opera, the Hartford Stage, the Hartford Ballet, and the Hartford Symphony) draw more than 700,000 people downtown annually. Their combined economic impact is more than $100 million.
- The Hartford Civic Center is a downtown fixture that has offered Greater Hartford an extraordinary blend of retail shopping, dining, sports, family entertainment, ice skating spectaculars, trade and consumer shows, concerts, and other special events for more than 20 years. By itself, the civic center pulls better than 1.5 million visitors to downtown Hartford each year.
- More than 300,000 people, 40 percent higher than projected, attended concerts at the new Meadows Music Theatre during its inaugural season in 1995.

Even more impressive, for every one of these examples, there are many more. People aren't just coming to Hartford, they are flocking.

The fact that Hartford is a safe city has a lot to do with why people are coming downtown. Parking, in both surface lots and high-rise garages, is plentiful, convenient, and, by big-city standards, affordable. Downtown is well lit. And police officers are apparent everywhere.

Police and city leaders have worked together closely to deal with crime. Early in 1995, they launched a program called the Comprehensive Communities Partnership, and it soon became clear that their efforts were having a positive impact.

The most immediate impact of the program was on the crime statistics. Overall crime in downtown Hartford is down by 45 percent from 1989 levels. Violent crimes have declined by more than 35 percent in the city's central marketplace. And property crimes have been reduced by nearly 47 percent.

■　　■　　■

Hartford has done a lot to change its style of policing, says Deputy Police Chief Tom O'Connor, who runs the downtown service substation on Pearl Street, home of the Hartford Police Museum. "We've moved from a very traditional form of policing to an approach aimed at community satisfaction."

That new approach is what the Comprehensive Communities Partnership is all about. And it is having a significant impact on crime throughout Hartford. Indeed, the partnership is built on "capturing the city, neighborhood by neighborhood."

"The partnership relies on three legs," says O'Connor. "For it to work, the people in the community, the police, and other government agencies must work in cooperation."

Critical to the partnership is citizen involvement. "The people who live in Hartford, work in Hartford, and visit Hartford deserve to feel safe," says O'Connor. "In turn, we depend on the people who live and work here to help us tackle crime.

"The residents of a neighborhood are most immediately in touch with what goes on there. We need to hear from them, and we need their support. The police can

"*T*HE GUIDES ARE ONE OF THE FIRST FACES OF DOWNTOWN HARTFORD THAT MANY VISITORS WILL ENCOUNTER, AND IT'S ALWAYS A POSITIVE FACE."

—AUSTIN JORDAN, DIRECTOR, HARTFORD GUIDES

help them deal with crime, and other government agencies can help them attack the structural problems that lead to crime and deterioration. Together, we are making Hartford a better, safer city."

Throughout Hartford, this innovative model for community betterment has begun to take root in myriad forms—cleanup and beautification efforts, Police Athletic League programs to reach young people before they fall victim to the scourge of gangs and drugs, grassroots neighborhood programs to reclaim the streets—and the positive results have quickly become apparent.

A key element in the effectiveness of the Comprehensive Communities Partnership model has been the designation of three police service areas, each staffed by a deputy chief. This strategy ensures that there is a concentrated police presence in each of Hartford's major areas—the North End, the South End, and downtown. Everywhere you go in Hartford, merchants and community leaders report seeing a more high-profile police presence—and less crime.

O'Connor attributes much of the decrease in crime to the increasing mobility of the police. A squad of officers mounted on bicycles, for instance, has made it possible for more police to be in more places more of the time.

"Our success also depends on effective communications," says O'Connor. The department has taken steps to improve communications with residents and to work more effectively to ensure community satisfaction with the level of service being delivered. In the downtown area this includes building a communications network with the private security organizations serving downtown companies, merchants, buildings, and organizations. Already, the police are well on the way to completing a comprehensive radio link with all members of the Security Corps Access Network (SCAN), the organization of downtown corporate security forces.

■   ■   ■

Credit for Hartford's increasingly safe and hospitable downtown doesn't go to the police alone, however.

Since 1991, the police have had a lot of help from a novel program called the Hartford Guides.

The Guides program was created in 1991 as a collaborative effort of the Hartford Downtown Council, an arm of the Greater Hartford Chamber of Commerce, and Business for Downtown Hartford, an independent organization of businesses dedicated to promoting the downtown retail area. The Guides are housed in the police department's downtown service substation, and on average they help more than 12,000 people every year.

"We like to think of the Guides as goodwill ambassadors," says Austin Jordan, who heads the program. "They are one of the first faces of downtown Hartford that many visitors will encounter, and it's always a positive face. There's really nothing the Guides can't help you with. You want to know where to buy a specific gift? You're looking for a certain kind of restaurant? You're lost? Whatever your problem is, the Hartford Guides are equipped to help."

The Guides are walking repositories of information about Hartford and the region. Professionally trained, they are highly knowledgeable about Hartford's history, geography, and attractions. They can provide directions to any-place in the region, as well as information about events, attractions, facilities, shopping, and dining.

Dressed in khaki slacks with red windbreakers and jaunty red golf caps, the Guides not only are unmistakable but seemingly are ubiquitous. Though there are only seven of them, they are constantly on the move, patrolling 26 square blocks of downtown Hartford. Every Guide covers as much as 11 miles in an eight-hour shift.

The Guides also function as an extension of the police department. All of the Guides are CPR certified and equipped with radios that link them electronically to the Hartford Police Department. They are also available as escorts for downtown workers and visitors in any kind of weather.

Hartford citizens also enjoy the safety benefits that come from having one of only 15 fire departments in the country with a Class 1 rating. That rating, bestowed on the department by Commercial Risk Services, a subsidiary of the

A Hartford Guide assists a visitor to downtown Hartford.

Hartford is not only a safe city to visit. It's also an easy city to visit.

Getting to and from Hartford and traveling around the Greater Hartford area are both easy, thanks to top-notch transportation systems. Indeed, given Hartford's enviable location, roughly equidistant from Boston, New York, and Albany, transportation is certainly one of the region's biggest assets.

Hartford is conveniently situated at the intersection of two of the major interstate highways serving New England. By car, it is only 2 hours from Boston and 2 1/2 hours from New York City. And with the multiple exits from both I-91 and I-84 into Hartford and surrounding communities, the area's superhighway grid is convenient for commuters, visitors, and commercial vehicles alike.

Hartford and nearby communities are served by Connecticut Transit's excellent bus system, which has more than 30 commuter and local routes, all of which converge along Main Street within walking distance of Hartford's downtown attractions.

Augmenting this system are Scooter buses. Throughout each workday, these buses arrive downtown every 10 to 30 minutes, providing a convenient option for workers who need to get crosstown for meetings or to take care of midday errands.

More than 4,700,000 passengers travel by plane each year from Greater Hartford's world-class Bradley International Airport, 12 miles north of Hartford in Windsor Locks. Sixteen passenger airlines operate an average of 300 daily domestic and international flights out of Bradley.

Traveling from Bradley will be even more convenient, as will commuting to Hartford, when a 15-mile light rail line between Hartford and the airport is completed. The rail line is also expected to be a boon to economic growth along the I-91 corridor.

Hartford's historic Union Station Transportation Center, a century-old brownstone structure that has been restored to its original Victorian beauty, serves as the hub of the region's rail and bus lines. Within walking distance of downtown Hartford, in the heart of the Arts and Entertainment District, the station is served daily by Amtrak trains connecting to major locations coast to coast and by several interstate bus companies that provide long-distance passenger service. Taxis and airport limousines also operate from the station.

The railroad station in the Hartford suburb of Windsor.

Bradley International Airport, located 12 miles north of Hartford, in Windsor Locks.

Insurance Services Office, is a reflection of the department's preparedness in several different categories.

"We have 17 companies in 12 stations covering the 18 square miles of the city," says Chief Robert E. Dobson. "We're an aggressive fire department."

The department responds to more than 23,000 calls each year and, on average, reaches a fire within three minutes of the call. As a result, an impressive 98 percent of the fires in Hartford are extinguished in their room of origin. The Class 1 rating alone saves Hartford commercial businesses an estimated $9 million in insurance premiums annually.

■ ■ ■

But safety is not the only issue confronting those who strive to promote use of a major urban center. Hartford Proud & Beautiful, another collaboration of the Hartford Downtown Council and the City of Hartford, was created to tackle the issue of cleanliness. It has succeeded admirably.

"Abandoned property, misplaced waste, litter, and debris make our city unattractive and create an overall negative impression for residents, workers, and visitors alike," says Anthony Caruso, president of Hartford Proud & Beautiful. "The focus of the organization is to keep the city clean; develop public and private partnerships for beautification projects; and educate and heighten the awareness of people on the importance of the cleanliness of the community."

Seven days a week, Hartford Proud & Beautiful crews clear walks, streets, and public spaces of litter and debris. Expending more than 12,000 hours per year, the crews collect more than 100 tons of trash.

The organization also has played a leadership role in the development of other initiatives. For instance, it has been instrumental in creating innovative educational and awareness programs to encourage students, residents, workers, and visitors to help keep the city clean. It functions as a center to facilitate the formation of public-private partnerships to sponsor and initiate beautification projects. It

uses public relations to boost public awareness and confidence about existing and proposed beautification and capital improvement projects. Finally, the organization offers classes and career planning services for its employees.

To expand the program's impact, Hartford Proud & Beautiful introduced an increasingly successful Adopt-a-Block program aimed at recruiting Hartford businesses to accept responsibility for maintaining, cleaning, and beautifying the spaces surrounding their buildings and properties. Each year more companies are signing up.

Hartford Proud & Beautiful has worked with a number of other organizations, including the Hartford Downtown Council, the Greater Hartford Chamber of Commerce, the Hartford Parks and Recreation Department, the Connecticut Prison Association, area garden clubs, merchant associations, and civic groups, to implement one of its beautification programs, called Hartford Blooms.

Inspired by a program in Hartford's Irish sister city, New Ross, each year Hartford Blooms seeds downtown Hartford with more than 500 two-foot-tall terra cotta planters filled with colorful flowers. "One would have to be blind to beauty to miss the more than 15,000 marigolds, impatiens, and zinnias painting downtown with their bright golds, pinks, and purples," wrote *The Hartford Courant* in an editorial applauding the project when it was introduced. Nearly all of the program's funding comes from private sources.

Day after day, block by block, projects like these and effective collaborations between citizens groups, business organizations, and government are making Hartford a better place in which to live, work, and play.

Quoting the plan that launched the Comprehensive Communities Partnership, Deputy Police Chief O'Connor says, "Public safety is the foundation without which no other activity can occur. People will not attend community meetings, let their children play in the parks, or dine in Hartford restaurants in the evening unless they feel they can do so without fear of violence or crime. We aim to make sure people feel safe here."

Downtown Hartford is safer these days, thanks to an extensive police presence, including a bicycle unit and a mounted patrol unit, shown here escorting the University of Connecticut's championship women's basketball team during a parade.

CONSTRUCTION AND REMEMBRANCE:
HARTFORD'S ARCHITECTURE

*M*aster woodworker William Gould helped
breathe new life into the Old State House
during its $12 million restoration.

e shape our cities, and then our cities shape us," wrote Winston Churchill. If he was correct, then the people who live and work in Hartford are unquestionably in the process of being changed. All over Hartford, the city is taking on a new shape architecturally.

Today's changes are not driven by trends as staggering as the steam-driven Industrial Revolution of the 19th century or as sweeping as the revitalization that seized the urban imagination in the 1970s. The changes taking place in Hartford now are more subtle, nothing like the architectural movements that left such indelible stamps on the landscape of the city as Samuel Colt's Armory, with its eccentric blue "onion" on top, or Armsmear, the stunning Italian villa that Colt built on Wethersfield Avenue in 1857. Nor are buildings being erected like the massive Travelers Tower, the 527-foot spire that is one of the most distinctive features of the Hartford skyline, or Aetna Life & Casualty's Farmington Avenue headquarters, the world's largest colonial-style building.

In the long run, however, Hartford's new landscape, and the forces driving its creation, may have as enduring an impact on the city as the Puritan ethic and Yankee ingenuity had in the past. As surely as it is

creating the commercial, educational, and informational resources of tomorrow, Hartford is building the city of tomorrow, too.

What's going on here seems more like the architectural realization of the themes that have made the First Night Hartford celebration a model for broad-based community festivals (and, incidentally, helped increase attendance at that event by more than 200 percent in its first four years). Hartford is experiencing a revolution in the development and management of public space.

Consider, for instance, the reclamation of the riverfront and the effect it will have on Hartford and East Hartford, long separated by artificial barriers not only from each other but from the river. Similarly, Bill Faude has supervised the renovation of the Old State House guided by the principle that this great building should be a gathering place for a citizenry increasingly engaged in reigniting the idea of community and rediscovering its ancient and restorative power.

These are only two examples of the vibrant architectural changes taking place here. Citywide there are examples of emerging spaces and places that seem to rejoice in the inextricably entwined ideas of people and possibilities.

The new pavilion in Bushnell Park, for instance, offers both a tribute to Hartford's love affair with parks and a permanent statement about Hartford's enthusiasm for public entertainment. Then there's the charmingly off-kilter geometry of the new Connecticut Children's Medical Center, a glass sanctuary inside which the voice of childhood sings about the immutability of the human spirit. These are places that nurture life.

One of the best examples of the architectural changes taking place may be the Main Street Market. Positioned at the head of the completely renovated Pratt Street, in downtown Hartford, the market has emerged as a breath of open air. Its barnlike buildings offer pleasing visual diversity among the towers of Main Street. Area farmers sell their produce here. People build things. The seeds of community take root in simple interactions.

*A*bove: Interior of the Old State House. Right: The Connecticut State Capitol.

The striking conservatory at the Mark Twain House, a National Historic Landmark and one of
the most beautiful homes in Connecticut.

With its permanent stage, the market has become an open-air center for diverse artistic expression. Every week, lunchtime visitors are treated to entertainment ranging from comedy to jazz to zydeco.

The Main Street Market is also the site of some of Hartford's most important and most diverse festivals and cultural events. The enormously popular Taste of Hartford, New England's largest food festival, attracts more than 150,000 downtown visitors during 36 hours of continuous entertainment in the market every June. In August, the market sways to the rhythms of calypso and reggae during Hartford's West Indian Festival.

"We try to save buildings in Hartford and create partnerships that will help to preserve Hartford's historic structures by making them viable and productive," says Michael Kerski of the Greater Hartford Architecture Conservancy, which manages the market. "The market is a good example of constructive preservation and use of public space." The conservancy has managed more than $30 million in projects over the two decades since it was founded.

Apply Churchill's perspective to Hartford today and you will discover a city engaged in learning about what author Mike Greenberg calls "the poetics of cities." But make no mistake, the poetry of Hartford's architecture is not written only in the rhythm and rhyme of its new public spaces. Many of the poetics result from the interface between new and old.

Across the street from the market, for instance, is the Cheney Block. Designed by Henry Hobson Richardson and built in 1876 under the supervision of his young associate, Stanford White, the Cheney Block's romanesque style and multiple levels of increasingly smaller arches could not possibly be in greater architectural counterpoint to the market. And there is magic in their juxtaposition.

■　　■　　■

But just as Hartford is creating a new architecture, it is determined to preserve what remains of its proud

heritage. One such place is Mark Twain's house on Farmington Avenue. With its incredible ornamentation and clever use of several architectural traditions, Twain's home is one of the most beautiful in Connecticut and a National Historic Landmark.

Twain's home is also the centerpiece of Nook Farm, the remarkable literary epicenter of many of the greatest voices of the 19th century, including Twain's and Harriet Beecher Stowe's. Nook Farm stands not only as a memorial to these literary giants but also as a memorial to a time when Hartford was a publishing center. In the mid-19th century, Hartford had some 20 publishing houses. The first American cookbook and the first American children's magazine were published here. And Noah Webster, who created the first American dictionary, made his home in West Hartford.

Historic buildings throughout Hartford are, like the Mark Twain House, inextricably tied to the region's past. They reflect not only diverse architectural tastes and styles but the cultural trends that have shaped Hartford over the past three and a half centuries.

"Hartford has a wealth of great architecture," says David Ransom, coauthor of *Structures and Styles: Guided Tours of Hartford Architecture*. "Any number of people could develop lists of the preeminent buildings. No two lists would necessarily be alike."

Nevertheless, it doesn't take him long to compile a list of buildings from the more than 500 in his book.

■　　■　　■

After the Mark Twain House and the aforementioned Cheney Block, which Ransom calls "the finest building in Hartford," his list contains the Day-Chamberlin House. Another component of Nook Farm, it sits next door to the Mark Twain House and was built in 1881 by Frances H. Kimball for prominent Hartford attorney Franklin Chamberlin. It is, says Ransom, "one of the architect's two great statements of the Queen Anne style in Hartford." The other is the ornate Goodwin Building downtown.

Next on Ransom's list are the offices of the Phoenix Mutual Life Insurance Company, a major Hartford landmark on Constitution Plaza often referred to locally as the "Boat Building." Built in 1963, it was designed by Harrison & Abramowitz and is, says Ransom, "Hartford's finest design in the international style."

Next is the Church of the Good Shepherd and its parish house, designed by Edward Tuckerman Potter and built in 1869 and 1896, respectively, on Wyllys Street in the South End. Potter's church, says Ransom, is "a skillful exercise in . . . high Victorian Gothic, resplendent with brightly patterned masonry, slate roof, and handsome interior."

Ransom's next entry is the Long Walk at Trinity College, which renowned architectural historian Henry-Russell Hitchcock called "perhaps the best example anywhere of Victorian Gothic collegiate architecture." The Long Walk was designed by prominent English architect William Burges, the only foreign architect ever known to have designed buildings in Hartford.

The next three entries on Ransom's list are government buildings—the Connecticut State Capitol, the Hartford Municipal Building, and the Connecticut State Library and Supreme Court Building.

The capitol is the only high-Victorian Gothic state capitol in America. Designed by Richard Michell Upjohn, it was built in 1878 after a protracted dispute between Hartford and New Haven over which city should be the state capital.

The design for the Hartford Municipal Building emerged from an architectural competition stipulating that the new structure should resemble the Old State House. Ransom draws particular attention to its three-story central atrium, which he describes as "one of the city's finest interiors, decorated with a wealth of classical detail and with panels depicting scenes from Hartford's history."

Ransom calls the Connecticut State Library and Supreme Court Building, constructed in 1910, a "monument to the city beautiful movement" of the early 20th century. It is "Hartford's most impressive beaux-arts classical building," says Ransom.

On Lewis Street, downtown, Ransom identifies five late federal/early Greek revival-style brick houses that are "the last surviving group of mid-19th-century residential structures in downtown Hartford."

Ransom selects a "charming cottage" built around 1875 at 121 Holcomb Street in the Blue Hills neighborhood as the next entry on his list. It is, he says, "the best example in Hartford of the stick style. Its high visual appeal arises from the board-and-batten siding and from the ornamental treatment of wood in the facade, in the canopies over the doors, and in the gables."

The final entry on Ransom's list is the unique residence built in 1930 on Scarborough Street in the West End for A. Everett "Chick" Austin, the director of the Wadsworth Atheneum from 1927 to 1945. "The house is only one room deep," says Ransom, "which, given Austin's dramatic flair, creates the not-inappropriate feeling of a stage set."

As Hartford strives to build a multicultural community for tomorrow and construct the public spaces for that community, it seems, more and more, to be

*R*ight: The historic Horace Bushnell Memorial Hall.

remembering the words of John Ruskin. Asked if it was expedient to preserve the buildings of the past, he said, "We have no right whatever to touch them. They are not ours. They belong partly to those who built them and partly to all the generations of mankind who follow us."

■   ■   ■

No city can create an environment in which dreams can breathe and hopes can take root without open spaces. Buildings and construction must enhance the overall aesthetic balance of the city, but there must be room for sunshine as well.

Thanks in large part to a remarkable man named Horace Bushnell, Hartford is not only a city full of outstanding buildings but a city blessed with a network of fine parks.

Less than 150 years ago, mills, factories, and tanneries, and the rundown tenements of the people who worked in them, lined the banks of the Park River, which flowed downhill from the current site of the state capitol on its way to its confluence with the Connecticut River at Dutch Point. Bushnell, a prominent Congregational minister and civic leader, was upset that this was the first view of Hartford visitors had as they disembarked from trains at the nearby station.

Determined to change the situation, in 1850 he launched a campaign to acquire the land and turn it into a park. He never could have imagined how difficult it would be.

Bushnell first had to convince city fathers to pass an ordinance making it possible for the city to acquire land by eminent domain to create parks. Then he had to muster support for his vision of a central park for the city.

This quest would occupy him for much of the rest of his life. Indeed, it took four years after the city's aldermen agreed that Hartford could acquire the land before the citizens of Hartford agreed to do so in 1854. Even then, the park was not a sure thing.

Rev. Bushnell was forced to be away from Hartford for two years. When he returned, in 1856, he was astonished to find that there was still no park. Indeed, the United States would be on the brink of the Civil War before landscape architect Jacob Weidenman would finally begin turning Bushnell's dream into a reality. The park Weidenman created, a sweeping lawn that rolls downhill along the river's course toward the center of the city, was the first in the world to be voted for and paid for by the citizens of a city.

Weidenman went on to become an associate of the renowned Frederick Law Olmsted, who was born in Hartford but did not work on Bushnell Park. Olmsted did, however, serve as a consultant during the development of many other parks in the city's expanding system, including Riverside, Goodwin, and Pope parks.

On February 14, 1876, the city council voted to change the name of the park Horace Bushnell had envisioned to Bushnell Park in recognition of his monumental contribution to the improvement of Hartford. Two days later, Rev. Bushnell died.

His legacy lives on, however. Thanks to the Bushnell Park Foundation, which preserves and maintains the park, Bushnell Park is used every year by thousands of Greater Hartford citizens for a wide range of community activities. And the 12 major and 24 minor parks in the Hartford Park System that began with Rev. Bushnell's dream now provide more than 2,150 acres of breathing space for the people of Greater Hartford.

Above: The Knox Parks Foundation greenhouse in Elizabeth Park. Right: The cupola of Goodwin Square.

Forty-eight Horse Power

In the northwest corner of Bushnell Park, in a vortex where time stands still, a herd of 48 splendid ponies prance through a timeless circle of light and color.

Haunting music compels these horses to run. All who hear that music must see the gallant racers. All who see them want to ride them. And all who ride them fall quickly under their spell.

The Bushnell Park carousel was built in the waning days of the ragtime era by Stein and Goldstein, the Brooklyn, New York, firm that built New York City's Central Park carousel. Long neglected, poorly fed, and run hard, the horses were in sorry condition and had lost their rhythm when the Knox Parks Foundation rescued them from a Canton, Ohio, amusement park in 1974 and had them shipped to Hartford.

Over the next two years, artist Tracy Cameron lovingly restored them to their original condition. At the same time, a search party found and restored an early 20th-century Wurlitzer band organ, because the horses could neither run nor fly without the music.

Then noted Hartford architect Jack Dollard designed a new home for them—a unique pavilion with no foundation, resting on 24 concrete piers and illuminated by 96 stained-glass windows decorated with scenes of the changing seasons.

And, in 1976, the band that had played while young men set out to fight the Great War once more struck up the beat. And the forever-young horses began to run again.

They still do. Year after year.

And sometimes, late at night, when all the city sleeps, they break out of the circle of their fate, slip the bonds of time, and caper among the fireflies, in the warmth of a Victorian summer, innocent and free.

*B*ushnell Park was the first park in the United States to be paid for by the citizens of a city and is now the site of a wide range of community activities, including outdoor concerts and events, held in a new pavilion.

*T*he governor's mansion, decorated for the holidays.

The sun sets on a pick-up basketball game in Elizabeth Park.

A detail from a wrought-iron fence on South Green.

$\mathcal{H}$artford is blessed with a network of fine parks, including Bushnell, the largest, and Colt Park (upper right).

*G*olfers enjoy
the links in
Keney Park.

*T*he rose garden
in Elizabeth Park is
one of the finest
in America.

A splash in one of the area's many public pools is a great relief from summer heat, or you can cool off in a fountain, like the one below in Goodwin Park.

GREATER HARTFORD:
HARTFORD'S DIVERSE SUBURBS

*W*oody Scott produces a wide variety of fruits
and vegetables on his farm in South Glastonbury.

he diversity that makes Hartford so exciting is not limited to the central city. Although Hartford is far and away the largest municipality in the region, only 125,000 people make their homes in the city, while nearly 1 million people live in the Greater Hartford area.

To appreciate the range of opportunities the region has to offer, one must get to know the towns scattered up and down both sides of the Connecticut River Valley. From tiny Andover, with a population of 2,500, to New Britain, a city in its own right, with more than 75,000 residents, the Greater Hartford region is made up of 32 remarkably varied communities.

■   ■   ■

Just west of Hartford is West Hartford. With 60,000 residents, it's the third most populous community in the region, after Hartford and New Britain. Fittingly, West Hartford, the birthplace of Noah Webster, is an educational center. The University of Connecticut's Hartford campus, St. Joseph College, the University of Hartford, and the American School for the Deaf are all located here, as is the popular West Hartford campus of the Science Museum of Connecticut. Embracing several neighborhoods, West Hartford enjoys a diverse business base as well as a wide range of residential areas. In recent years West Hartford Center, directly west of Hartford along Farmington Avenue, has become a noted dining area, where restaurants serve many different cuisines.

Beyond West Hartford, the traveler crosses a ridge of land that rises diagonally across the center of the state. In the Greater Hartford region, its west side is the watershed of the Farmington River, a lazy stream that snakes back and forth in leisurely twists and turns across its old and fertile delta.

The Farmington is one of the most popular recreational rivers in the area. It is fished extensively. On hot summer afternoons, hundreds of people jump into inner tubes at Satan's Kingdom State Park and float along with the current.

The towns along the river are some of the oldest in Connecticut. Avon, Canton, Farmington, Simsbury, Granby, and East Granby are popular bedroom communities, and each has its own special flavor.

Avon, with a population of 14,000, has both tree-lined neighborhoods and a vibrant central commercial district on Route 44, the old "Albany Avenue" route that used to take travelers from Hartford west toward Albany, New York. Avon Old Farms School, a prominent preparatory school, is located here.

Canton, west of Avon, has many residential areas, as well as a bustling business district along Route 44. It is the home of the popular Roaring Brook Nature Center.

The town of Farmington is south of Avon and eight miles west of Hartford. With a population of more than 20,000, Farmington is the largest community in the Farmington River Valley. It is home to the headquarters of Otis Elevator and the University of Connecticut Medical School's Health Center. The late Jacqueline Kennedy Onassis was the most famous alumna of Miss Porter's School for Girls, whose campus is just off the main street, in Farmington's historic district.

Simsbury, north of Avon, is an upscale residential community with growing commercial and industrial districts. Talcott Mountain State Park, along the rocky spine that bisects central Connecticut, attracts visitors who want to see the 165-foot Heublein Tower, former home of the Heublein family, founders of the liquor bottling company, which is headquartered in Hartford. From the observation deck at the top of the tower, visitors can enjoy spectacular, panoramic views of both sides of the ridge. On clear days it is possible to see as far as Springfield, Massachusetts.

In the flat, fertile fields of Granby and East Granby, one can still see the red tobacco barns that have long been pictured in Connecticut tourist periodicals. Situated northwest of Hartford, Granby and East Granby remain what they've always been, farming communities. Both towns were settled in the 17th century and today have a combined population of just under 15,000. Many residents commute to jobs in the Hartford area, but many still work in farming, raising dairy cattle, tobacco, and vegetables. Granby is home of the 4,300-acre McLean Game Preserve, one of the largest preserves in Connecticut.

$\mathscr{I}$n autumn, the
Greater Hartford area is
a wonderland of color.

Outdoor recreation is an
important part of life in
Greater Hartford. Trout
fishing in Spice Brook Pond
in West Hartford is a great
way to enjoy an afternoon,
as are tubing and canoeing
on the Farmington River
(page 124).

Bloomfield, just minutes north of Hartford, has a population of nearly 20,000. A commercial and industrial center, it continues to attract new business but is a popular residential area as well.

Farther north are the towns of Windsor, Windsor Locks, Suffield, Somers, and Enfield. Established in 1633 as a farming community, Windsor was the first English settlement in Connecticut. Although agriculture remains an important part of the economy of this Connecticut River town, Windsor has a growing business and industrial base. More than 60 companies are located here. Like many towns in the region, Windsor is also a residential community and the home of several significant historic sites, including the birthplace of Oliver Ellsworth, the nation's third chief justice.

Windsor Locks, also along the banks of the Connecticut, is a thriving community with a healthy mix of residences and retail and commercial establishments. Its economy has benefited from being the home of Bradley International, the major airport serving Greater Hartford.

Suffield and Somers, northwest and northeast of Hartford, respectively, are small communities that historically were farming villages. Somers is home of the James F. King Indian Museum, which houses a large collection of Native American artifacts as well as memorabilia from the French and Indian, Revolutionary, and Civil Wars.

Once a Shaker community, Enfield is a prosperous farming and industrial town near the Massachusetts border. With more than 45,000 residents, it is a popular regional shopping center.

East of Hartford, on the opposite side of the Connecticut River, are East Hartford, South Windsor, Manchester, Tolland, Vernon, Andover, Coventry, Hebron, Marlborough, Ellington, and East Windsor, collectively referred to locally as "the East Side."

East Hartford, with more than 50,000 residents, is the fifth-largest town in the region. Like West Hartford and New Britain, it is a self-contained city. East Hartford's primary employer is the jet engine manufacturer Pratt & Whitney, which, with thousands of workers, is one of the largest employers in the region. An active participant in the Riverfront Recapture project, East Hartford has many residential neighborhoods and is home of the Edward F. King Museum, which tells of the development of tobacco farming, aviation, and other area industries.

Once a farming community, South Windsor retains some of its rural charm. The town also has attractive residential neighborhoods and a vigorous, growing business and commercial district.

Manchester, with nearly 53,000 residents, is the region's fourth-largest town. In addition to being a popular residential community, this former mill town has become a major shopping center. It also has industrial parks, a hospital, a community college, many historic homes, the Lutz Children's Museum, and 215-acre Wickham Park.

Once agricultural communities, Tolland and Vernon, east of Manchester, have 10,000 residents and 29,000 residents, respectively, and are growing. Many people in these towns are employed by United Technologies Corporation and the University of Connecticut. Many others commute to Hartford but still benefit from the advantages of country living. Vernon has a growing industrial and commercial base and is the home of Rockville General Hospital. Tolland has many famous historic sites, including the colonial Benton Homestead and the 1856 Tolland Jail Museum.

Coventry, Hebron, and Marlborough are quiet residential communities situated in picturesque countryside east of Hartford. Coventry, whose lake attracts summer visitors, is the birthplace of Revolution patriot Nathan Hale. Hebron, 20 miles southeast of Hartford, is home of Gay City State Park. Like Coventry, Marlborough has a lake that is used recreationally.

Ellington's convenient location, northeast of Hartford, has made it a popular community. Its residents benefit from Crystal Lake and other recreational facilities.

Rural East Windsor has enjoyed steady growth both industrially and residentially in recent years. It is the home of two popular regional attractions, the Connecticut Trolley Museum and the Connecticut Fire Museum.

South of Hartford, Glastonbury and Wethersfield both boast large historic districts. Glastonbury, on the opposite side of the Connecticut River from Hartford, has many buildings dating from as early as 1693. From Rocky Hill, a residential community and the site of Dinosaur State Park, where the footprints of three-toed Jurassic dinosaurs are preserved, one can cross the Connecticut River to Glastonbury on the oldest continuously operating ferry in the United States.

Old Wethersfield, a historic district in the town of Wethersfield, contains the town's 17th-century burying ground and some 150 restored 17th-century homes and buildings. It claims to be the "most ancient towne in Connecticut."

With a population approaching 30,000, Newington, south of Hartford, is primarily a residential community. It is the home of the Newington campus of the Connecticut Children's Medical Center and of the Veterans Administration Medical Center.

Just west of Newington is New Britain, which has its own hospital, symphony orchestra, minor league baseball team, and university, Central Connecticut State. An important regional industrial center, it is the home of world-famous Stanley Tool Works.

■   ■   ■

What do these communities offer Greater Hartford?

For starters, they offer a tremendous range in housing possibilities. Within the Greater Hartford region, the prospective homeowner has a wealth of options from which to choose. In the mid-1990s, the average price of a single-family home in the region was $183,300, but prices ranged from $120,000 to $130,000 in some communities up to more than $200,000 in others.

The choices in housing design are equally extensive. Authentic brownstones, comfortable apartments, high-rise condominiums, historic 18th- and 19th-century houses—they're all available in Greater Hartford,

in settings that range from quaint villages to upscale suburbs.

Recreational opportunities abound as well. The directory of the Greater Hartford Chamber of Commerce lists nearly 100 recreational amenities in Greater Hartford's suburban communities. They include historic sites, art museums, educational facilities, nature centers, historic homes, theaters, sports arenas, and many other attractions.

Finally, these communities add strength and vitality to the region's economy. Although many of the towns surrounding Hartford are essentially bedroom communities, others have strong commercial districts that have enjoyed considerable growth in recent years and are expected to grow rapidly in the years to come. Manchester, for instance, has benefited from the development of popular malls that attract shoppers from throughout the area. And Windsor has attracted more than 40 companies in the past few years through a concerted economic development incentive program, resulting in the addition of three new jobs daily during that period. And thanks to programs like the Capitol Region Partnership, these towns are likely to continue experiencing growth in the future while finding more efficient ways to collaborate on their shared needs.

In short, these communities offer a diverse range in residential and recreational options, as well as a growing economic base that will continue to thrive as the Greater Hartford region redefines itself and builds for the future

Golfers can choose from more than 50 courses in Greater Hartford.

When the first snow arrives, kids head for the hills.

Some evenings and weekends you can't find a place to park in the first lot at the Metropolitan District Commission's (MDC) Reservoir Number 6, off Route 44, halfway up Avon Mountain between West Hartford and Avon. You have to drive down by the water treatment plant at the far end of the reservoir.

Along the way you pass walkers, joggers, bikers, roller skaters, rollerbladers—a parade of people using simple modes of transportation.

Reservoir Number 6 is one of the most popular recreational sites in the Greater Hartford area. On warm weekend days, thousands of people hike or jog around the reservoir's easy three-mile perimeter path.

The trail around Reservoir Number 6 is well maintained and affords hikers and joggers alike a pleasant opportunity to commune with nature in close proximity to some of Greater Hartford's more populous areas.

Three miles south of Reservoir Number 6, the network of trails around the MDC's Reservoirs Numbers 1, 3, and 5, just off Farmington Avenue, also is popular with hikers and nature lovers. It's an easy hike from Farmington Avenue through the woods to Avon Mountain, and even though these paths are heavily used, there is plenty of room for everyone. In fact, although the trails are practically within shouting distance of West Hartford, Avon, and Farmington, one is as likely to encounter a deer or a cluster of jack in the pulpit flowers as another hiker.

THE HOLCOMB FARM PROJECT

A lot of great stuff is growing on the 325-acre Holcomb Farm Estate, the former home of prominent Granby residents Tudor and Laura Holcomb, who bequeathed their property to the town.

Each year, during the summer, the Holcomb Farm is the setting for an experiment in agriculture, environmentalism, and community, one of three such projects in Connecticut. The program is coordinated by the Friends of the Holcomb Farm, Inc., and by the Hartford Food System, an organization that distributes free food to Hartford's poor and elderly residents.

Here's how the program works. Several acres of the farm are planted with arugula, beans, beets, broccoli, cabbage, cantaloupe, carrots, cauliflower, collards, and perhaps 40 other vegetables, fruits, and herbs. Shares of the produce are bought by families in Granby and by Hartford organizations. Each week during the growing season, shareholders come to pick up their allotted portion of the produce, which is grown organically. The shareholders also spend time working as volunteers on the farm, gardening and in the process learning about each other.

One-Chane, a North End community group, also brings inner-city teenagers to the farm each week, where they have an opportunity to work outdoors in fresh air and to learn the enduring lessons of the land, stewardship, responsibility, and the cycles of life.

The Hartford Food System provided the funding to launch the program. The organization's goal is not only to make food available to Hartford residents but to make the project self-sustaining and, in so doing, to restore the link between people and agriculture.

During the first season of the project, more than 32,000 pounds of produce were grown and distributed. Poor and elderly people in Hartford enjoyed fresh, nutritious fruits and vegetables grown in the region. People in the suburbs and from the inner city who might never have met worked side by side, learning about those aspects of their lives they have in common. And youngsters from impoverished Hartford neighborhoods discovered the magic that grows in gardens.

$\mathcal{S}$ights reminiscent of an earlier era are common in rural Connecticut, like this street sign in Wethersfield and this horse farm in Colchester.

Many homes in Hartford's suburbs offer the convenience of country living within a short distance of the city.

The Hill-Stead Museum in Farmington has one of the area's finest collections of impressionist art and hosts the Sunken Garden Poetry Festival.

The Heublein Tower, in the distance, tops a scenic vista for visitors to Riverdale Farms in Avon.

Tobacco barns are still a common site in the rich agricultural land of Bloomfield.

Following pages: West Hartford Center.

*R*ight: The Hartford skyline as seen from Wickham Park, on the East Hartford/ Manchester border.

A New Kind of Government

Lillian Banks, shown in the Legislative Office Building, is a sessional worker in the Bill Room of the Connecticut General Assembly.

artford and government—you can't separate them. Blame it on that most "congregational" of men, the Rev. Thomas Hooker.

In 1636, Hooker led a party of 100 men, women, and children on a quest for religious freedom from Massachusetts to what would become Hartford. It could only have been an arduous trip. There were no roads, just wilderness. But Hooker was a determined man.

What he founded here was a reflection of that determination. On May 31, 1638, two years after Hooker's party dug in on Connecticut soil, he gave a sermon in which he outlined the basic tenets of what led to the Fundamental Orders, the legal document that established Connecticut's first government. It is generally conceded to have been the world's first written constitution.

It is a tribute to Hooker's philosophy that Connecticut is called the "Constitution State." And, for the most part, the business of government in the state has remained a tribute to his philosophy as well. The foundation he laid was both simple and enduring.

Hooker believed that "the foundation of authority is laid in the free consent of the people" and that "the privilege of election belongs to the people." And since "God hath given us liberty," people should take advantage of that liberty.

Hooker also believed in the essence of Puritanism.

He had not led his band of followers through primeval forest and swamps because he had any abiding doubts about human nature.

The society Thomas Hooker created was predicated on the notion that humans were basically flawed. Their only hope of salvation was through devotion to God and work and uncompromising adherence to a rigid philosophy. The Puritans were a hard, unbending people. But they lived, and ultimately survived, under hard, unforgiving circumstances.

Although Rev. Hooker and many of his followers died in an epidemic in 1647, his colony and the philosophy on which it was built continued to thrive. And generation after generation, Connecticut's citizens internalized a set of basic ideas about life that were reflected in the kind of government they created.

They believed that man was not irremediable so long as he worked hard and lived a disciplined life. They also believed government ought to serve the collective needs of a community. Most of all, these newcomers believed in independence and the need to take responsibility for oneself. They were, after all, Yankees.

■   ■   ■

Two hundred and sixty years later, Hartford remains the capital of Connecticut. No visitor to Hartford could miss that.

Thomas Hooker probably would have thought that the massive Connecticut State Capitol with its gilded dome was ostentatious. But there's nothing ambiguous about it. If buildings had voices, it would shout, "Government!" and the word might sound like "Permanent!"

There have been changes, though. And one of the most significant is taking place right now.

As other communities sprang up around the colonial center that Rev. Hooker established, at first called Newtown, they created in their own local governments that same Yankee independence that Hooker and his followers brought with them from the Massachusetts Bay Colony. Indeed, any description of

the attributes of local governments in New England would certainly mention their autonomy.

In Greater Hartford, however, if that autonomy is not crumbling, there certainly are some cracks. How the governments within the region (from the state government to the government of Hartford to the governments of the surrounding communities) interact these days is changing significantly.

As the costs of government continue to rise, these communities are discovering that the costs of rigid autonomy may be too heavy to bear. They also are discovering that it is possible to let their diversity work to their mutual advantage.

So, they are changing. And the direction that change is taking is toward regional cooperation.

■   ■   ■

There is no better symbol of the change taking place than the Capitol Region Partnership. "People love their local government," says West Hartford's mayor, Sandy Klebanoff, who chairs the Partnership. "They love to have government accessible to them. The trouble is, it's also very expensive. More and more, intergovernment cooperation is becoming an economic necessity. The Partnership is an effort to get the key players in the region together to solve problems."

Created in 1995, the Partnership is a collaboration of the Capitol Region Council of Governments (CRCOG), the Capitol Region Education Council (CREC), the Connecticut Capitol Region Growth Council (CCRGC), the Metropolitan District Commission (MDC), the Capital Region Workforce Development Board (CRWDB), and the Greater Hartford Transit District (GHTD). Right from the start, the Partnership began to demonstrate its value, says Klebanoff.

"Job training is a great example," she says. "Often in the past it hasn't been very successful, because

people were being trained for jobs that didn't exist. But with the Partnership in place, all the players are sitting down together and discussing how to do things effectively. Instead of just training people, the Workforce Development Board and the Growth Council are studying where the jobs are and where they are going to be in the future, so that we can train people for those jobs."

Klebanoff points to job development as a related issue. "The Greater Hartford area was hit hard by the recession," she says, "but we're coming back. We're determined to retain and stimulate jobs in the region."

Each of the organizations in the Partnership has a stake in that objective. CREC is the regional education organization, charged with ensuring that Greater Hartford residents get the education and training they need to prepare for the future. CRWDB has the job of developing the workers that regional businesses in a reborn economy will need. CRCOG is the municipal arm, helping Greater Hartford governments solve their problems, including business development and employment, collaboratively. MDC has the job of building the infrastructure of the future.

"There's a lot of wasted effort if we all tackle these issues separately," says Klebanoff. "By working together we can help each other to solve problems more effectively and more efficiently."

𝓛eft: The Escher-esque floor of the Legislative Office Building's main rotunda. Above: Hartford's mayor, Mike Peters, and some of his "kids."

Throughout the area, government leaders at all levels are finding synergy an increasingly attractive idea. The Capitol Region Partnership is only one example of what can happen when it exists.

More and more, town managers and other local government leaders are reviewing their municipal budgets and looking for ways to trim costs. When Avon, for instance, eliminated its health department in 1993 and began to contract health services from the local health district, the town saved more than $100,000.

"There's no question local citizens like their local government," says Avon town manager Phil Schenck, an active member of CRCOG. "We're all having to adjust to a new paradigm, though. I think you'll see much more of this kind of collaboration in the future.

"People want to be able to set the standards in their local communities, but I think you'll begin to see many services provided regionally. If several towns can contract services like trash removal or snow plowing more economically by working together, it doesn't make much sense to buy those services individually."

Schenck believes the role of local governments will not disappear entirely. "There will still be local citizen access points for services," he says.

Wethersfield town manager Lee Erdmann agrees. He has been instrumental in the development of a strategic economic development plan and a marketing plan for Wethersfield that use Hartford's revitalization efforts as an engine for regional revitalization.

Like Schenck, he believes intergovernment collaboration through organizations like the Capitol Region Council of Governments and the Capitol Region Partnership makes a lot of sense. "Reducing the costs of local governments by finding more efficient ways of providing the services we all rely upon will free funds for the important job of building for the future," he says.

Schenck and Erdmann, and many of their counterparts in other Greater Hartford communities, are quick to praise the outreach efforts of Hartford mayor Mike Peters. Since his election in 1993, Peters, an active supporter of regional cooperation, has visited the towns of Greater Hartford to foster the relationships on which regional collaboration depend.

Connecticut governor John G. Rowland supports regional cooperation, as well. "Frugality will always be a hallmark of this administration," says John Chapin, a spokesman for Rowland. "The governor is enthusiastic about any kind of sensible, functional approach to regional government cooperation. Many of the programs going on in the Greater Hartford area right now make a lot of sense. In the long run, these efforts to reduce the cost of government and find joint solutions to problems should benefit the overall growth of the Greater Hartford area."

Not that this plan is easy. The theoretical benefits of synergy aside, one would be hard put to find a government leader in the region who is entirely comfortable with the notion of regionalism.

But that's how it is with change. No one knows exactly what's going to happen. But they know that the alternative to regional cooperation is less efficiency and greater expense.

*G*overnor John G. Rowland

*G*reater Hartford students learn about government in action at the Connecticut State Capitol.

*T*he rotunda of the Connecticut State Capitol.

$\mathcal{T}$he elegant architecture of Hartford City Hall.

"When public housing was created, its purpose was to provide safe, decent, and affordable housing for the working poor," says John Wardlaw, executive director of the Hartford Housing Authority. "It was transitional housing. It supported the family unit and family values. The underpinnings of public housing were directed toward self-sufficiency."

A man on the street outside Wardlaw's office is pushing a rusty shopping cart full of redeemable cans and other treasures. A block away, a Conrail engine blasts its horn twice as it thunders across Flatbush Avenue heading south. Just down the street, railroad spur lines that once served thriving businesses in an industrial age are overgrown with weeds.

"Wouldn't it be great if we could put those trains to use supporting this project," says Wardlaw, spreading a map across his desk. The project he is talking about could eliminate much of the blight of Charter Oak Terrace, a notorious public housing complex on the border between Hartford and West Hartford.

Built in 1941, the 1,000 units in Charter Oak Terrace were slated for demolition in the 1950s, but 40 years later they are still standing. Over the past two decades they've become a black hole, sucking up millions of dollars for repairs.

Only 700 units currently are occupied. The others are uninhabitable. Nearly all the residents are unemployed and receive some form of public assistance.

Thanks to a $45 million federal grant, Wardlaw has an opportunity to turn Charter Oak Terrace into what may be a national model for public housing. His plan is to eliminate many of these decrepit buildings and replace them with single-family homes that could be rented with an option to buy. A floodplain of the nearby Park River will be turned into a community recreational area. And the plan will convert a large chunk of the property into an economic development park, with the intent of employing area residents and breaking the cycle of poverty that grips the Terrace.

Wardlaw knows something about poverty. He grew up in the rural South, one of 16 children.

"Poverty is a state of mind," he says. "It's the incubator of all other social ills. If you build for the poor, then you perpetuate poverty by denying people the self-initiative and drive to improve their lives."

Wardlaw has met with Hartford and West Hartford business leaders to discuss the sort of businesses that make the most sense for the new complex. The Capitol Region Growth Council, a regional public and private development agency, is expected to produce an economic development strategy.

Charter Oak Terrace abuts commercially zoned land where existing businesses will likely benefit from the economic development. It also has the advantages of access to Interstate Highway 84 and the main railroad line serving Hartford.

"The idea here is to give people a chance to improve their lives and become productive citizens," says Wardlaw. "This plan opens up a real business opportunity while addressing a significant problem. This plan aims to do something about poverty."

EPILOGUE

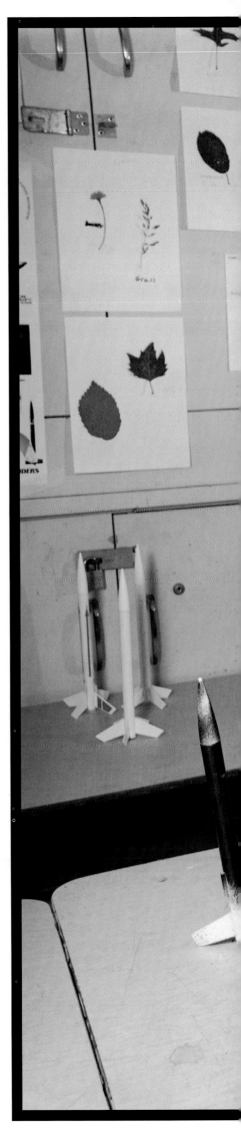

Selina Diaz, of Windsor, looks to the future as
a participant in Project EQUAL at Hartford's
Bulkeley High School.

Late night, August 23, 1995.

And so it ends—the journey I began in an airplane over Hartford untold hours of research, countless interviews, and thousands of words ago.

I set out to discover something called cultural diversity in the late-20th-century state of mind called Greater Hartford as I left terra firma on that bright, sunny morning in April. I also embarked upon a search for something worthy of celebration as this 350-year-old social experiment nears the millennium. More important, I hoped I'd find hope.

As I look back on the last four months, I know there is no reason I should not have expected to find hope here. Hope has been an essential ingredient of every brick laid and every cubic yard of concrete.

People in Greater Hartford know how to dream—not merely to noodle grandiose ideas but to envision the future and then rally the resources to make that future happen. They have had three and one-half centuries of practice.

A man named Hooker dreamed here of a constitutional form of government in which the inherent freedom of all men was a given.

A woman named Stowe dreamed of a rustic cabin

and a great cause that captured the imagination of a nation.

A man named Webster dreamed of a uniquely American tongue, the only correct language for expressing an idea as big as America.

A man named Gallaudet dreamed that the deaf should not be deprived of an education because of their affliction.

The oldest public art museum in the United States has existed here for more than 150 years. The first painless dentist, Horace Welles, discovered anesthesia here. The oldest newspaper in the country has been published here without interruption since 1764.

You don't have to look far to find dreams in Hartford. In the darkest corners of this city, I met people who cradle the light of life in their hands and never let it die, no matter how cold and bereft of hope the world around them sometimes seems.

This is a region of tough people. And each day they tenaciously reclaim this place. They do so because hope is not passive. Nor is it a given.

Hope takes root where people believe that the arts can save the children of inner-city poverty from a life of hopelessness. It grows where people from many backgrounds come together to tend the soil and plant seeds and wait for the rain.

It grows where citizens refuse to let their city be stolen by criminals. It flourishes where people with vision can see the possibilities in reclaiming a river, rebuilding an old state house, creating a medical center for children, reaching out to businesses and helping them help themselves to prosperity.

Hope grows wild here—in vacant lots, on windowsills, in the cracks in the street. And it will continue to thrive here, because the people who live here know how to dream.

In my refrigerator, downstairs, there is a bottle of sparkling wine that has been chilling for four months. I have saved it for this evening, for my own private celebration of Greater Hartford's cultural diversity. I'm

going to open it now and pour a glass and offer a toast to the future of this remarkable place.

Listen:

In 1988, the Capital Region Education Council launched an innovative summer program called Project EQUAL for middle school youngsters from all over the Greater Hartford area. One of its goals was to provide a learning environment in which youngsters could discover Hartford's roots and the contributions of various ethnic groups to the region's rich cultural mix. Another goal was to create a social program in which youngsters from the inner city and the suburbs could interact and test the veracity of negative cultural stereotypes.

For several weeks each summer, kids meet to learn about each other, share ideas, wrestle with the problems and issues confronting urban America, and experience the inimitable joy of having the doors in one's mind unlocked and opened. They learn things that will serve them, and the region, well when they grow up. More than anything, they learn what diversity can mean in the broadest sense, from appreciating other cultures to appreciating new ways of imagining what a truly great place Greater Hartford is on the way to becoming.

One of the students who participated in Project EQUAL in the summer of 1995 was 13-year-old Beth Marchessault of South Windsor. While she was a student in the program, Hartford's Arts and Entertainment District was growing up right before our eyes. The Connecticut Children's Medical Center was under

construction. The riverfront was less than two years from being completely recaptured. The bold new future of Greater Hartford was unfolding every day.

As Project EQUAL was winding down for the summer, someone asked Beth what she thought the best thing was about Greater Hartford and what she would like the region to be like when she grew up.

Here is what she said:

"I believe the best thing about the Greater Hartford area is its culture, and the remarkable differences between its citizens. Hartford is an extremely multicultural city, almost as much so as New York City. To become successful in the future, the Greater Hartford area must strive to remain multicultural. Children must learn to celebrate their differences, not despise them.

"Right now I can take steps toward making my dreams come true. I can make one park litter-free. I can educate one person about racism. The little things I can do sure can add up to one big change."

Here's to you, Beth. Dream on.

ENTERPRISE PROFILES

We constantly hear the age-old phrase "It takes a whole community to raise a child." Along those lines, it takes a whole region to support businesses. For nearly 200 years, the Greater Hartford Chamber of Commerce (GHCC) has done just that—and so much more—serving as one of the leading business organizations in the region.

The mission of the Greater Hartford Chamber of Commerce is to advance the civic, economic, and cultural interests of the people of Greater Hartford. Each year the GHCC continues to take its mission one step farther.

"What we do goes way beyond what is expected of a chamber of commerce. We really touch the lives of people in the region," says Mary Hart, a member of the GHCC Board of Directors and Executive Committee.

The Greater Hartford Chamber has become known throughout the country for taking the lead on issues that extend beyond the traditional boundaries of business, knowing that economic prosperity does not exist in isolation of other facets of life in the region the GHCC serves.

The month of April 1995 found the GHCC's president, Timothy Moynihan, "down and dirty," raising a slanting, sinking porch from below for an elderly Hartford homeowner as part of the national housing rehab program "Christmas in April." Two months later, GHCC staff and many member companies took to the city streets for the third year in miniature Grand Prix-style race cars to benefit Junior Achievement of Greater Hartford. One month later, GHCC members collected food for Foodshare's "Feed a Child" program,

and annually the GHCC joins hundreds of local companies by contributing to the United Way/Combined Health Appeal campaign.

Not a month goes by that the GHCC does not participate in, assist, or sponsor some function or cause. That's just how it is. That's just how the GHCC defined its mission.

"We really try to address the human and social issues," says Hart. "We deal with labor issues, education, economic development, housing, health care, transportation, human services, quality of life, entertainment, downtown development. All these things set us apart from business lobbying firms."

Social issues are only a small piece of the grand contributions the GHCC has made in recent years. It has been viewed by many as the "initiator." And when good ideas, leadership, and resources are needed, the GHCC is the natural source. The GHCC takes pride in putting good ideas to work—and businesses take pride in knowing that they can trust the GHCC to do so.

One of the GHCC's most recent, successful initiatives has been the formation of the Capitol Region Partnership, a voluntary collaboration of dedicated, regional groups that have agreed to work together for the betterment of the region. The GHCC also spearheaded the formation of one of the partners—the Connecticut Capitol Region Growth Council—an economic development corporation that has been working to bring new business to Greater Hartford, retain old business, and help existing companies grow.

"The only way you can get people to

Enjoying a summer excursion on the Lady Fenwick, *sponsored by Riverfront Recapture, are Roger Gelfenbien, managing partner, Andersen Consulting, Inc., and chairman of Hartford Proud & Beautiful, a program of the Hartford Downtown Council; Timothy Moynihan, president of the GHCC; Mary Hart, a member of the GHCC Board of Directors and director of public and community relations, CNG; and Thomas Groark Jr., chairman of the GHCC and partner, Day, Berry & Howard.*

© Kim Sirois

work for an organization and develop a product is if that product is going to be used," says Thomas Groark, Jr., chairman of the GHCC. The products of today are regional initiatives and cooperation, not only in Connecticut but across the country. A city is only as strong as its region, and the region cannot survive without its core—the city.

"Neither one can operate independently," says Hart. "Major employers still sit in downtown Hartford. That interdependency is still there."

The Capitol Region Partnership is made up of the Capitol Region Council of Governments, the Capitol Region Education Council, the Connecticut Capitol Region Growth Council, the Metropolitan District Commission, the Capital Region Workforce Development Board, and the Greater Hartford Transit District.

"We are always striving to make the region a better place to do business. Standing alone we cannot compete economically. And I think everyone has recognized we have to do something," says Moynihan. "It is something that cannot be taken for granted, something that will not simply take care of itself. Forming partnerships like this one pools resources, creates efficiencies, and enables the region to work toward one common goal—to improve the quality of life in Greater Hartford."

Another significant commitment the GHCC has made in its efforts to maintain a vibrant business community is lobbying at state legislative and local government levels. Through public affairs activities, the GHCC maintains a strong presence at the Hartford City Hall and at the Connecticut State Capitol. And GHCC committees—State Legislation, Tax and Fiscal Policies, Government Affairs, Congressional Club, Local

First Night Hartford, managed by the Hartford Downtown Council, brings more than 30,000 people to the city to celebrate the new year.

Government, Advisory Council on the Environment, and Education—keep a close watch on spending, legislation, and policy issues on a daily basis.

As the country expands its focus globally, the vision at the GHCC also broadens. In recognition of the need to promote international trade more

actively, the GHCC recently reenergized the International Business Council. The GHCC has established commercial exchanges with Sherbrooke, Canada, and Queretaro, Mexico, for its members. It has also published, in conjunction with the University of Connecticut, two trade guides to Latin America.

"As the marketplace continues to expand, it behooves us to link our members to international companies. Chamber of commerces are trusted sources. We must use that common thread as a common benefit," says Moynihan.

"Ninety-five percent of the world's population lives outside the United States. Those are our customers," says Kenneth Butterworth, retired chairman of the Loctite Corporation, a GHCC member company.

With a glimpse toward the future, the GHCC also is active at the local level, both financially and technically, in educational initiatives.

"We know that the business community is a stakeholder in education. The quality of education and the educational outcomes of the communities' students are important to us if we are to employ these students in the future. We must support partnerships that bring business and schools together in collaboration,"

says Marie Massaro, chairman of the Education Committee.

In 1995, the GHCC formed the Hartford Public Schools Governance Team Executive Coaches Program. The coaches—volunteers from the GHCC's member companies—work hand in hand with 33 school governance teams made up of parents, teachers, administrators, paraprofessionals, and community members. In an effort to improve student performance, the coaches assist the teams in transferring the tools of Total Quality Management into school environments.

Although considered a large chamber of commerce with its membership base of over 2,500 members, the GHCC caters to small businesses, especially through its Business Council. In fact, 80 percent of the GHCC's members are considered small to midsized businesses. Most have joined as a result of the GHCC's relationship with Affiliate

Chambers in the towns of Avon, Bloomfield, Canton, Farmington, Newington, Rocky Hill, Simsbury, and Wethersfield. Each Affiliate Chamber has its own board of directors and is given direct representation on the GHCC Board of Directors.

"This is a group of people acting collectively," says Jack Muirhead, president of the Board of Governors, Affiliate Chambers, and of New King, Inc., of Wethersfield. "I stand by that old cliché, I guess: if you are not part of the solution, then you are part of the problem."

One of the best reasons businesses join the GHCC is the benefits—and each year the benefits seem to get better and better. In 1994, the GHCC formed the Benefits Center, which serves over 23 chambers of commerce in the region by offering health-care benefits, including dental, life, short- and long-term disability, and Section 125 plans, at competitive rates. GHCC's other membership benefits don't

Volunteers from the Greater Hartford Chamber of Commerce and the Hartford Downtown Council, as well as the Master's Construction Group of Avon, took part in the Christmas in April housing rehab program in Hartford.

fall short, either. Discounts are offered on sporting and cultural events and on cellular and long-distance phone services. In addition, there are hundreds of opportunities to network and a wide array of publications that reach thousands of readers each year, including the GHCC's newsletter, which is published monthly in the Business Weekly section of *The Hartford Courant*.

"Ask 20 chamber members why they joined and you'll get 20 different answers," says Moynihan. But probably the most frequently cited is the visibility that can be gained and the ability to make lasting business connections with other members. One particularly successful quarterly event inaugurated in 1995 is the "Breakfast of Business Champions," which has attracted such prominent figures as M. L. Carr of the Boston Celtics; Geno Auriemma, coach of the NCAA champion UConn women's basketball team; actress Susan Saint James; and Dallas Cowboys defensive backfield coach David Campo. Also during 1995, the GHCC sponsored the first Beasley Reece/GHCC Celebrity Golf Classic, which attracted sports greats such as Lawrence Taylor, formerly of the New York Giants, and André Tippet of the New England Patriots. The Women Executives Committee presented best-selling author and management guru Dr. Stephen Covey at a leadership seminar. And, of course, there are always the traditional chamber networking events, such as the Business Expo, the Government Reception, the A.M. Networks, and new-member receptions.

The GHCC founded an affiliate organization, the Hartford Downtown Council (DTC), more than 20 years ago to focus on downtown issues. The council's enthusiastic mission is to make Hartford

The GHCC and the Downtown Council sponsor numerous activities, including the 1995 University of Connecticut men's basketball blue-and-white scrimmage pep rally and game held at the Hartford Civic Center in November.

the economic, cultural, and educational center of the region—and its efforts are paying off. The Downtown Council has teamed up with the business community and the management of the Hartford Whalers to keep this vital economic force in our city. And in 1993, the Hartford Marketing Collaborative, a collaboration of over 80 arts and entertainment groups, neighborhood merchant associations, retail ventures, and promotional organizations, was formed. The Collaborative packages all that the city has to offer as an entertainment center, focusing on the retail and service industries.

The Downtown Council also brings thousands of people to the city streets through the events it manages or produces, such as Kid'rific, First Night Hartford, Festival of Light, and Taste of Hartford. The GHCC also increases the beauty and safety of the streets through the Hartford Proud & Beautiful program, the Hartford Guides, and the Safety Coalition Task Force.

"I personally think the central city is very, very critical to the region," says Edward Morgan, chairman of the DTC. "And the Downtown Council is making every effort to boost Hartford. There's really so much here. People just need to rediscover it."

Other affiliate organizations of the GHCC are Leadership Greater Hartford, a network of informed leaders from businesses and nonprofit organizations who form task forces to examine and develop solutions for timely topics in education, housing, youth, employment, health, and social services, and the Citizens for Effective Government, a group that helps city and state administrators improve the management and operation of government.

No matter where you turn, the Greater Hartford Chamber of Commerce is involved somehow, some way, whether it's through its member companies, volunteers, or staff. The GHCC has important work to do—to make sure those who live and work here are proud of the region they call home.

The City of Hartford under the leadership of Mayor Mike Peters has made great strides in preparing for the future. Mayor Peters has focused his administration on building bridges and fostering strong working relationships with all segments of the community—from neighborhood leaders, to the corporate community, to the surrounding towns and cities that make up Greater Hartford.

The hallmark of these advances has been the development of partnerships with both public and private organizations to address business development and community issues.

"Both residents and businesses are more positive about the future of our city," says Mayor Peters. "Our neighbors in the suburbs are more receptive to cooperating with Hartford on projects of mutual interest. And more and more people are coming to Hartford for leisure activities."

Mayor Peters points to a number of significant achievements that have contributed to this new urban vitality and optimism.

An infusion of $5.4 million in Justice Department funding has enabled the city to beef up law enforcement. As a result, crime in Hartford is down.

A $48 million federal grant is enabling the city to rebuild the Charter Oak Terrace public housing complex. The project is a cooperative effort involving all levels of government and innovative public-private collaboration. Tied to an economic development park that will generate jobs for residents, the project is expected to become a national model for public housing.

Greater fiscal conservancy and more efficient management of city services have enabled the city to cut taxes while delivering the same or better quality services.

"Everywhere you look in Hartford these days, you see partnerships and collaboration," says Mayor Peters. "We're revitalizing the city, creating jobs, attracting new businesses, helping existing businesses to grow, creating better housing, and improving the overall quality of life.

"What all of this means is opportunities. We're opening up new opportunities for the people who live here, work here, and do business here. And we're also opening up opportunities for new people to come to Hartford for recreation or to make a greater investment in a region with enormous potential. It's an exciting time to be here."

Courtesy of City of Hartford

Mayor Michael P. Peters

THE HARTFORD STEAM BOILER INSPECTION AND INSURANCE COMPANY

In the mid- to late 19th century, during the Industrial Revolution, the Connecticut River was alive with steamboats. Steam drove the great turbines on land, too, in the boilers of the city's burgeoning factories.

Despite its potential dangers, steam was the most important energy source for industries throughout America. Its greatness as a power source was matched only by the enormity of the devastation it caused: in the 1850s, a major steam boiler explosion occurred every four days. Many people in America believed that boiler explosions were acts of God, no different from floods or earthquakes.

In 1865, the steamboat *Sultana* exploded on the Mississippi River, killing more than 1,200 people. Shortly after the explosion—the worst boiler disaster in history—two young Hartford businessmen, Jeremiah M. Allen and Edward M. Reed, set up an organization to inspect and insure steam boilers.

Both men had been members of the Polytechnic Club, established in 1857 to study scientific phenomena and their practical utilization. Acting on club discussions of ways to anticipate and prevent explosions, Allen and Reed founded The Hartford Steam Boiler Inspection and Insurance Company.

When the company was incorporated on June 30, 1866, it became "the first institution in America devoted primarily to industrial safety," according to Allen, its first president.

Today The Hartford Steam Boiler Inspection and Insurance Company retains not only its original name, but, more importantly, its original mission. "We benefit businesses, governments, and industries worldwide by providing services and consulting in risk management, safety, reliability, and efficiency," says Gordon W. Kreh, president and chief executive officer. "Our equipment, process, and risk management specialists combine technical expertise, industry perspective, and information systems with the financial strength of Hartford Steam Boiler to help our customers avoid losses from equipment failure, recover promptly from losses that do occur, and realize the maximum return from their equipment and processes."

Specifically, the company offers engineering services and property insurance that help protect people, property, and the environment. The company's core business is equipment breakdown and property insurance for commercial and industrial facilities. Hartford Steam Boiler is the market leader in this business with approximately 40 percent market share.

Drawing on the dedication of its employees—more than 50 percent of whom are engineers and technicians—Hartford Steam Boiler applies engineering and advanced technology to

The headquarters of The Hartford Steam Boiler Inspection and Insurance Company at One State Street

Rotating equipment requires special attention to assure that it is operating within design limits.

help manage risk and solve the operational problems of businesses worldwide—because customers would rather avoid losses than be paid for them.

Hartford Steam Boiler's insurance operations are focused on serving the needs of two main customer groups—commercial and special risks. The Commercial Division addresses the equipment needs of small business, working through agents and brokers and with more than 100 multiline insurance companies. While boilers were once the mainstay of its business, today Hartford Steam Boiler's 170,000 commercial customers and their covered equipment may range from a dentist's water purifying system to a dry cleaner's steam boiler to a printer's four-color press to a law office's computer system.

The Special Risks Division provides specialized engineering and risk management services and consulting worldwide to machinery-intensive industries

such as power generation, manufacturing, and chemical, oil, and gas. Industry specialists work closely with these customers to design risk reduction and insurance programs specific to their needs. Hartford Steam Boiler's Engineering Department provides technical and consulting services to both the Commercial and the Special Risks divisions.

Companies of Hartford Steam Boiler include The Boiler Inspection and Insurance Company of Canada; HSB Engineering Insurance Limited, which provides equipment insurance and specialized engineering services to locations outside the United States and Canada; HSB Reliability Technologies, a reliability improvement consulting and services firm; HSB Professional Loss Control, a fire protection engineering consulting firm; and Radian Corporation, an international environmental, engineering, and technical services firm.

"With our risk management and engineering experience, Hartford Steam Boiler's goal is to use technology to realize efficiencies and add value to all that we do," President Kreh says.

"Technology today makes it possible for our engineer in China to have access to the same high level of information as our engineer in Chicago," Kreh explains. "This technology also provides our underwriters and customer service representatives—wherever they are located—with all the information they need to make sound decisions and serve customers quickly and efficiently."

From the steam engine that drove fly wheels and pulleys to today's computerized-control equipment, Hartford Steam Boiler has applied technology to help solve the problems of business and industry. And, celebrating 130 years of service in 1996, the company is ready to meet the challenges of the 21st century.

COOPERS & LYBRAND

Coopers & Lybrand L.L.P., founded in 1898, is a "Big Six" accounting, tax, and consulting firm whose Hartford office mirrors the dramatic changes that have taken place in the accounting profession in recent years.

One of 98 Coopers & Lybrand offices in the United States, the Hartford office adheres to the firmwide values of integrity, teamwork, mutual respect, and personal responsibility. Through these shared values, each of the firm's offices works to provide its clients with uniformly high quality.

C&L's multinational clients also are assured of receiving high-quality services, whether they are located in Singapore or Shanghai, London or Lucerne, Mexico City or Moscow. The staff's knowledge of the international business environment and cultures is enhanced through exchange programs, and C&L's technology—automated audit programs, groupware, and communications systems—enables worldwide engagement teams to communicate on a real-time basis with each other and with their clients.

C&L's highly sophisticated software programs also facilitate tax planning, support the preparation of feasibility studies, and enable clients to benchmark and identify best practices for their business processes.

TARGETING INDUSTRY-SPECIFIC NEEDS
Audit, tax, and consulting professionals are organized into industry groups to meet the specific needs of clients in many fields, including high technology, health care, manufacturing, insurance, banking, real estate, construction, and retail, as well as in not-for-profit and government agencies.

In addition, the firm's professionals are trained and experienced in meeting the unique needs of emerging business and middle-market companies in the areas of finance, business planning, technology, and human resources.

As authors of the most definitive document on managing business risk, *Internal Control—Integrated Framework*, published by the Committee of Sponsoring Organizations of the Treadway Commission, Coopers & Lybrand is widely regarded as the expert on internal control.

CONTRIBUTING TO THE COMMUNITY
Coopers & Lybrand takes seriously its responsibility to support the communities in which it does business. Realizing that the future business climate—and society as a whole—is in large part dependent on today's youth, in 1989 the firm "adopted" a class of inner-city high school students through Project BRIDGE. C&L Hartford office staff have supported, as mentors and tutors, 15 students through high school graduation. With financial aid provided by C&L, several of those students have pursued higher education, and two have received bachelor's degrees.

Coopers & Lybrand also supports the Inroads, Inc., program, which enables talented minority youth to intern with local businesses, and the Connecticut Pre-Engineering Program, which encourages minority students to pursue careers in math and science.

SOLUTIONS FOR BUSINESS
Whether meeting the needs of its communities, providing financial services, or monitoring federal and state regulatory and tax developments for its clients, Coopers & Lybrand provides the resources its slogan pledges it will give them: **Solutions for Business.**

AETNA LIFE AND CASUALTY COMPANY

Connecticut has been home to Aetna since 1853, when the company's first president, Eliphalet Adams Bulkeley, opened a small office in downtown Hartford. Today, Aetna is headquartered in the world's largest Colonial-style office building and is one of the nation's major shareholder-owned insurance and financial services organizations.

Aetna is one of the world's leading providers of managed health care services, property and casualty coverage, life insurance, and asset management. Strong, stable, and experienced, Aetna has earned the trust of millions of customers who rely on the company to help them build financial security and manage life's risks.

From its vantage point in Hartford's Asylum Hill neighborhood, Aetna and its employees understand that the company is linked to the surrounding community not only economically, but culturally and socially as well. Two-thirds of all Aetna employees participate in volunteer activities in their communities. The personal generosity of its employees is buttressed by Aetna's corporate public involvement programs and by the Aetna Foundation, Inc.

Aetna started its first "Saturday Academy" in 1984 in Hartford. Saturday Academy, which has expanded to seven other cities, is an education enrichment program for inner-city middle school students *and* their parents. In addition,

Aetna contributes millions of dollars to children's health and minority education initiatives. An innovative immunization tracking and monitoring system, created by the Hartford Health Department with support from the Aetna Foundation, is considered a national model.

Ronald Compton, Aetna's chairman, believes the time, effort, and resources the company and its employees devote to the community must continue to be one of Aetna's core values. "A community is nothing more—or less—than what its citizens decide it should be," Compton says. "We mold our community by our actions, our energy, and the way we treat each other."

Aetna's corporate headquarters, located on Farmington Avenue in Hartford

If you peruse the historical archives of Travelers Insurance, you will find two pennies dating back to 1864. Therein lies a fascinating tale about the company's origins.

The story goes that in March 1864 a Hartford businessman, James G. Batterson, met a local banker, James E. Bolter, in the post office. It seems Bolter had heard that Batterson and several partners were organizing a company that would introduce accident insurance to North America.

According to A *History of the Travelers*, Bolter inquired of Batterson, "I'm on my way home for luncheon. How much would you charge to insure me against accident between here and Buckingham Street?"

Batterson replied, "Two cents," whereupon he took two pennies from Bolter and tucked them in his vest pocket. Bolter walked home unscathed, and Batterson hung on to the two-penny premium, an important souvenir in the vast archives of the company founded in April 1864 by James Batterson.

Travelers has evolved significantly from the days of two-penny premiums. Today, Travelers Group is one of the largest and most profitable financial services companies in America.

The company's long-time emblem has been an umbrella, symbolic of its dedication to the protection and security of its customers. The distinctive red umbrella remains in evidence today, as does that sense of dedication.

What has changed is that Travelers is more than a company that protects customers against accidents. Travelers Group is now a diversified financial

Travelers Group is deeply committed to providing the best training and education resources for its employees, as well as for staff at outside companies and organizations. The Travelers Education Center is a 135,000-square-foot state-of-the-art conference center in Hartford. The center features 30 meeting rooms, four advanced IBM PC training rooms with LAN connectivity, a 180-seat amphitheater, and specially designed reception and dining areas.

services company engaged in investment services, consumer finance, and insurance services.

With the highest rankings for many of its business lines, Travelers Group also has achieved a dominant position in financial services. The company is a top-10 U.S. money manager, a top consumer finance company, a major life insurance and annuity provider, and a major provider of property/casualty insurance for institutions and individuals.

Through its commercial insurance business lines, Travelers is a leader in providing innovative solutions to workplace health and safety issues.

Besides being a strong, profitable company, Travelers is deeply committed to helping others through the Travelers Group Foundation, its philanthropic arm, whose annual budget exceeds $10 million. While education programs and early childhood care account for more than half the foundation's philanthropic efforts, Travelers also gives generously to the arts, health and human services, and civic organizations.

Travelers' philanthropic endeavors help nationally recognized organizations, such as Carnegie Hall and Head Start, but also local shelters and social service

The Travelers Tower is a landmark on the Hartford skyline.

agencies. Travelers also provides career training for the financial services industry, primarily through the Academy of Finance, which company chairman Sanford Weill was instrumental in founding.

From its origins as the first company in America to insure against accidents to its merger in 1993 with Primerica, Travelers has undergone profound transformation to ensure its position as a nationally prominent provider of insurance and financial services to tens of millions of Americans. Yet the company's mission has never wavered. James Batterson's two cents remain a powerful reminder of a 130-year commitment to helping companies and individuals achieve financial security in a rapidly changing society and marketplace.

Travelers is a leading provider of home, auto, and life insurance. Computer links with thousands of independent agents help the company better serve them and their customers.

In May 1810, the general assembly of the state of Connecticut adjourned. Most of its business had been routine. One act regulated how charcoal would be measured. Another forbade the removal of deceased persons "from their places of sepulture." Yet another was "an act to incorporate the Hartford Fire Insurance Company," now known as ITT Hartford.

This act empowered the new insurance company, one of the country's first, to "write insurance of every description, on goods, chattles, wares and merchandise, and other personal estate of every name, nature and description." The emergence of Hartford as "The Insurance City" had begun.

Events soon tested the company's mettle. Fanned by strong winds, a roaring fire destroyed much of New York City on December 16, 1835. As the city burned, a newspaper reported, "We take it for granted that the fire insurance companies are all ruined."

But the fire helped build ITT Hartford's reputation for financial strength, integrity, and dependability. The company's president, Eliphalet Terry, pledged his personal fortune as security, gathered a list of all ITT Hartford policies, ordered a sleigh and team of horses, and set out in a snowstorm for New York, where he paid claims in person and in full.

In the six-month period prior to April 1835, premiums totaled $19,260.15. But in the six-month period following the New York fire, premiums jumped to $97,841.75. A new era had begun.

■ ■ ■

ITT Hartford, the country's seventh-largest property and casualty insurer, had 1994 premiums of nearly $5.7 billion. ITT Hartford Life is one of the country's fastest-growing major life insurance groups and ranks as America's 11th largest, based on $43.2 billion in assets. The company has more than 20,000 employees worldwide.

ITT Hartford property and casualty operations write personal, commercial, specialty, and reinsurance coverages. The commercial market segment is the company's largest; more than 500,000 policies are written. The company also ranks as the nation's 10th-largest personal lines insurer. Over 6,000 property and casualty insurance agents sell ITT Hartford products in North America.

ITT Hartford Life provides individual and group life and disability insurance, as well as retirement planning products and services for individuals and employers, including corporations, municipal governments, and small businesses. These products and services are available from a variety of agents, brokers, and plan administrators.

■ ■ ■

ITT Hartford focuses on distinct market segments to achieve profitable growth in the highly competitive property

Hartford Plaza, headquarters of ITT Hartford Insurance Group, on Asylum Avenue, just west of downtown Hartford

The Hartford stag is among the oldest and most respected symbols of strength in the insurance business. Its first known use was on an ITT Hartford policy written in 1861 to insure Abraham Lincoln's Illinois home.

and casualty lines. Market segmentation enables managers to respond to customer needs with new approaches and products.

For example, small businesses make up the fastest-growing part of the domestic economy. Taken individually, few small businesses generate enough premium to pay for the custom-tailored insurance programs they need. But put them together in affinity groups, and they have the "critical mass" needed to give the creative thinking of ITT Hartford and its agents a workout.

HartRe, a subsidiary of ITT Hartford, is a worldwide provider of reinsurance, with operations in Hong Kong, Spain, the U.K., the U.S., and Canada. Its 1994 written premium of half a billion dollars places it among the largest reinsurers in the United States. HartRe offers a full portfolio of standard and specialty products and services to its

customers, primary property and casualty insurers.

ITT Hartford is the only agency company among the top-10 personal lines insurers.

In 1984, ITT Hartford was named the licensed provider of personal lines for the American Association of Retired Persons (AARP). Through telemarketing operations in Southington, Connecticut, and San Diego, California, the company has written more than $1 billion in new business and has penetrated only 6 percent of the market.

■ ■ ■

More than 700,000 Americans own ITT Hartford Life annuities, making the company the nation's leading seller of individual annuities in 1994. The company has been the leading seller of annuities through banks for the past five years.

New marketing arrangements have expanded the customer base of ITT Hartford Life. For example, through its majority-owned subsidiary, American Maturity Life, the company is directly marketing individual annuities to members of AARP.

Success in annuity sales illustrates the strategy of ITT Hartford Life—use financial strength and acumen to establish sustainable competitive advantages in key markets.

ITT Hartford Life has also staked out a strong position in the employee benefits market. The company has clients of all sizes but has recently focused on selling short- and long-term disability plans to employers with fewer than 300 employees. The growth potential in this market is significant, since small and midsized businesses account for 95 percent of all employers.

■ ■ ■

From its beginnings as a fire insurance company, ITT Hartford has grown into a premier provider of insurance and financial services with operations around the world.

In 1995, ITT Hartford became one of three independent companies spun off by ITT Corporation. Donald R. Frahm, chairman and chief executive officer of ITT Hartford, said, "When we were acquired by ITT almost 25 years ago, ITT Hartford was a well-regarded but modestly sized company, with assets just over $2 billion. Today, we are among the 100 largest companies in the United States.

"By any measure, we are a premier insurer, poised to take advantage of extraordinary opportunities around the globe. As we complete our second century of leadership in the industry, we begin an exciting new era."

B. PERKINS & CO., INC.

President Brewster B. Perkins

How does an insurance agency become an integral part of a diverse business community? Simple. It becomes involved and committed. It provides competitive products and services. It develops lasting relationships with customers, vendors, and others trying to make the community a competitive, productive, and fulfilling place in which to work and live.

B. Perkins & Co., Inc., prides itself on being as diverse and unique as the city and region it serves. Established in April 1980, this Hartford-based insurance agency services large corporations as well as many not-for-profit organizations.

Brewster Perkins, president of the agency, has 25 years of experience in the Hartford insurance industry. A graduate of Trinity College and the University of Connecticut's business school, he remains committed to keeping B. Perkins & Co., Inc., in Hartford. In fact, he recently relocated the company offices to the United Way building on Laurel Street, helping to revitalize an area formerly void of businesses. "It is an expression of our confidence in Hartford," he states.

B. Perkins & Co., Inc., provides property and casualty coverage, employee benefits, health, life, and personal lines insurance, and pension and retirement investment consultation. The company aims to produce synergy by building long-term relationships with businesses and individuals. The agency offers a wide variety of services, including loss-control analysis and risk management, as well as prompt, accurate claims processing.

The agency's success is exemplified by its management techniques, client base, and employees.

B. Perkins' employees have diverse professional backgrounds, including experience in the marketing of national and international companies, in the management of large accounts, in risk exposure analysis specific to nonprofits, and in the development of new and emerging computer techniques to enhance and complement personal service. The agency's vice president of sales has been the organizer and chief executive officer of a New York-based insurance company and has broad experience assessing the needs of financial institutions. The chief operating officer was an executive at a major national insurance company for several years. In addition to his organizational skills, he counsels in the areas of pension and retirement investment.

All of B. Perkins' employees are encouraged to continue their educations, to achieve advanced professional designations, and to join industry organizations. Participation, education, and communication are, in fact, at the heart of B. Perkins' management philosophy.

Photo by Diane Sobolewski Photography, Branford, Connecticut

B. Perkins & Co., Inc., is the insurance agent for the Hartford Whalers and other sports teams.

They also are central to the agency's perception of its role in Greater Hartford. Whether staff members are reviewing alternative markets for the unique risk exposures of a client or discussing fund-raising ideas for the United Way campaign, the agency has a commitment to excellence.

Both Brewster Perkins and his staff support and advise Greater Hartford human service agencies. Brewster Perkins maintains many long-standing professional relationships while also participating actively in community enterprises. He is past president and campaign chairman for the United Way/Combined Health Appeal. He is a member of the Distribution Committee of the Hartford Foundation for Public Giving, the ninth-largest community foundation in the country, and a member of the board of directors of the Coordinating Council of Foundations. In addition, recognizing the need for strong relationships and leadership, he has encouraged others to become involved and invested in Hartford.

All employees of the agency follow Brewster Perkins's lead, giving time and professional support to community organizations. The agency's entire staff served as volunteers at the Special Olympics World Games held in Connecticut in 1995, and employees have been strong advocates and supporters of the United Way's Day of Caring.

In addition to a large clientele of commercial businesses, the agency insures nearly 300 social service organizations. The agency's diverse client roster includes major sports teams, large international manufacturing companies, banks, real estate developers, schools, and museums. With clients around the globe, the staff of B. Perkins often travels internationally to assess client needs and offer solutions.

B. Perkins & Co., Inc., remains in Hartford by choice. "We're confident that the city will continue to adapt to economic and social changes and attract new business," says Brewster Perkins. "With a strong urban base, the entire region benefits."

The variety and texture of Hartford will always distinguish it from other locales. B. Perkins & Co., Inc., strives for distinction within the insurance industry and the community in the same way—by providing consistently professional service and by dedicating its resources to investing in the area.

B. Perkins & Co., Inc., based in Hartford, has clients around the globe.

When Fleet Bank merged with Shawmut National Corporation in 1995, the result was an $80 billion institution. With more than 25 percent of those assets, Fleet's Connecticut bank immediately emerged as the largest in the state.

Under the leadership of Richard A. Higginbotham, president and chief executive officer, the bank aims to continue growing by providing the complete scope of financial services Connecticut businesses require as the state's economy is being shaped for the future.

"Being the state's largest financial institution is both a privilege and a responsibility," says Higginbotham. "Connecticut has enormous potential, and Fleet has a major responsibility to help promote and develop the tremendous resources available to businesses here. Accordingly, our fate is closely tied to the future of Connecticut and Hartford."

One of the bank's major priorities is to help retain businesses in Connecticut and to collaborate with government and business leaders to attract new businesses.

"It's not enough anymore to simply provide consistent assistance and service to businesses," says Higginbotham.

"We must continue to be innovative. We must understand and anticipate the needs of the businesses already in Connecticut and those that will move here and develop here in the future."

Higginbotham emphasizes that the bank's responsibility to the state's businesses includes small and midsized companies as well as major corporations. "We will continue to be a major lender, assisting the small businesses that are an increasingly important segment of the economy," he says. "We are also extremely interested in providing products and services to low- and moderate-income families. During the last few years Fleet's Connecticut staff has worked with community leaders to develop effective community reinvestment programs and products. I'm especially pleased that in 1995 their efforts were recognized with an Outstanding rating, the highest grade from the Office of the Comptroller of the Currency. We intend to maintain this rating by continuing to achieve the highest levels of performance through creative programs, leadership initiatives, and superior products and services."

Fleet also makes a significant contribution to Connecticut through philanthropic and volunteer programs. A major donor to civic, artistic, and charitable organizations, the bank focuses especially on programs supporting children and education. More than 1,000 Fleet employees volunteered for the Special Olympics World Games, held in New Haven in 1995.

Courtesy of Fleet Bank

President Richard A. Higginbotham

In 1990, Saint Francis Hospital and Medical Center contracted with International Managed Care Strategies to develop a hospital-based statewide preferred provider organization (PPO). That network, HealthChoice of Connecticut (HCC), was launched on October 1, 1990.

HCC is a for-profit corporation separately incorporated from its sponsoring organizations. Fifty percent of HCC stock is owned by the Camillus Corporation, the parent company of Saint Francis Hospital. Yale New Haven Hospital, located in New Haven, owns the remaining 50 percent of the stock.

In today's business environment, every employer must balance the desire to provide benefits to employees with the need to contain costs. With its superior reporting capabilities and experience in plan design, HealthChoice works with companies to develop and refine their plans for the greatest possible savings without reducing benefits so that employees become dissatisfied. HealthChoice can work with companies of any size and can offer both self-funded and fully insured products.

One of the largest PPOs in the region, HCC covers more than 150,000 lives. Subscribers benefit from an extensive provider network, with physicians in every medical specialty. HCC offers a choice of more than 4,000 physicians, 1,800 ancillary providers, 29 hospitals, and 400 pharmacies.

While HCC's provider network is unusually large, subscribers are not limited to picking a network provider. HCC strongly believes in subscriber choice.

In addition to its extensive provider network, HCC manages claims administration and utilization management for its subscribers. HCC's state-of-the-art utilization management program is designed to examine the medical necessity of services carefully to ensure that all patients get the highest quality of care, while guaranteeing that costs are managed effectively for subscribers.

To meet the growing needs of employers, HCC is continually introducing new products. This gives the company the ability to offer an even more expansive product line with variable costs and designs. As a result of these new products, HCC has become one of the fastest-growing PPOs in the region, adding an average 1,000 lives per month.

CONNECTICUT CAPITOL REGION GROWTH COUNCIL AND CONNECTICUT ECONOMIC RESOURCE CENTER, INC.

The Connecticut Capitol Region Growth Council is a not-for-profit corporation that resulted from a collaboration of business and government leaders. Its purpose is to retain and strengthen businesses already based in Greater Hartford and to recruit new businesses to the region.

Since its inception in 1992, the Growth Council has helped preserve and create more than 2,500 jobs in the Capitol Region by launching several important initiatives. Among them are the Business Visitation Program; a plan to increase intertown cooperation; and a regional development strategy. An innovative economic assistance program, METROFUND, has resulted from these initiatives.

METROFUND, the first program of its kind in Connecticut, is designed to support the retention and expansion of existing businesses and the relocation of new businesses to the region. METROFUND's site readiness component supports companies involved in many kinds of construction projects. Another aspect of the METROFUND program is a revolving loan fund to help area companies with limited ability secure loans from existing commercial funding sources. Loans can be used for a wide range of improvement projects.

The Connecticut Economic Resource Center, Inc. (CERC), is a nonprofit, private-sector organization formed and managed through a unique partnership of utility/telecommunications companies and state government. Since its incorporation in 1993, CERC has served as a one-stop, comprehensive source of information for businesses and economic development professionals. Its mission is to promote Connecticut as a prime business location.

CERC coordinates Connecticut's business-to-business marketing and recruitment efforts on behalf of the state. It works to create a more positive, responsive environment for companies doing business here or businesses that are interested in relocating to or expanding in Connecticut. These activities are coordinated through a partnership between CERC and the state's economic development agencies.

CERC provides a variety of products and services, including SiteFinder, a computer database of Connecticut's available commercial and industrial properties, and the Business Resource Index, a database of programs and services for businesses; CERC also consults on a contractual basis, providing marketing and communications planning and services for economic development organizations.

ConnectiCare, headquartered in Farmington, has been a leader in the managed care market in Connecticut for the last 14 years. The company's leadership position has been bolstered by its strong commitment to the employers, people, and medical community in the state. With over 2,500 covered companies, 145,000 covered members, and over 4,000 participating providers, ConnectiCare's commitment has been rewarded.

During 1994 and 1995 alone, ConnectiCare's leadership position has been validated through:

- an HMO member satisfaction rate in excess of 97 percent for five straight years;
- an employer renewal rate of higher than 95 percent; and, finally,
- recognition of the company, through an independent survey conducted by *Medical Economics* magazine, as the managed care organization with the highest satisfaction among physicians. In fact, many physicians, as well as hospitals, are covered by ConnectiCare's plans, and hundreds participate in its ongoing training programs.

ConnectiCare believes that the company succeeds because ConnectiCare cares. The company cares about managing the cost of health care effectively for its business clients, and it cares about providing flexible options to meet the needs of their employees. For this reason, ConnectiCare offers an entire portfolio of managed care products, including HMO plans, point-of-service plans, and self-funded EPO plans.

Courtesy of ConnectiCare

Providing reasonable access to doctors and hospitals has also been an imperative for ConnectiCare. During 1994 and 1995, the company expanded its network statewide and into Hampden County, Massachusetts, so that it now has 24 hospitals and a total of over 4,000 other providers in its network.

ConnectiCare cares about its members and wants to provide them with services and benefits that make them satisfied while still helping to control costs for their clients. All of the company's health plans include preventive care, wellness programs, and its FitCare health club program. Additionally, through its customer service department, ConnectiCare contacts new members by phone or postcard to ensure that they understand the plans and the services available to them. Customer relations representatives are available on an ongoing basis for questions and guidance.

ConnectiCare has consistently earned an HMO member satisfaction rate of 97 percent for the past five years.

ConnectiCare cares about its clients, who will not accept compromised service for the sake of a few dollars in savings. The company's account management process focuses on the needs of its customers. The company has also invested significantly in the systems necessary to reduce administrative costs while enhancing overall service.

ConnectiCare products are available through the Chamber Insurance Trust through participating Chambers of Commerce and their participating Chamber agents. ConnectiCare's products are also available through other agents representing ConnectiCare. Businesses with over 100 employees can customize their plans on a self-funded basis through ConnectiCare's Health Management Corporation affiliate.

It stands only a short distance from the Connecticut River, and to most people it looks like a large boat. Known as the world's first two-sided building, the Hartford home office of Phoenix has become an area landmark.

Founded in Hartford in 1851, Phoenix is the 14th-largest mutual life insurer in the United States. The current company was formed by the merger of Hartford-based Phoenix Mutual Life Insurance Company and New York-based Home Life Insurance Company, the largest merger ever of two mutual life insurers.

A MUTUAL COMPANY OWNED BY POLICYHOLDERS

As a mutual company, Phoenix is owned not by stockholders but by its more than 400,000 policyholders. Phoenix is dedicated to helping people find solutions to their insurance and investment needs throughout their lifetimes. The company takes great pride in knowing that individuals, families, and businesses look to it for innovative products and superior service.

The company offers a diverse portfolio of personal and business life insurance products, as well as employee benefit programs, individual investment products, institutional investment management plans, reinsurance, products designed for international markets, and property-casualty insurance through a network of agencies.

Phoenix matches its concern for insuring the financial well-being of policyholders with a strong commitment to improving the quality of life in Hartford and other communities where the company conducts business. That commitment shows in its business investments, corporate contributions, volunteerism, community leadership, and corporate sponsorships.

In 1995, Phoenix merged its investment operations with Chicago-based Duff & Phelps, creating a new publicly traded money management company headquartered in Hartford, named Phoenix Duff & Phelps. This new company further positions Phoenix as a significant contributor to the Greater Hartford economy.

Also in 1995, the company's property-casualty brokerage subsidiary, American Phoenix, merged its Kenney Webber & Lowell agency with another Connecticut-based agency, Goodwin, Loomis & Britton. The merged agency, called American Phoenix of Connecticut and based in downtown Hartford, is one of the largest property-casualty agencies in New England. American Phoenix is among the top-20 property-casualty agency networks in the country.

A POLICY OF COMMUNITY SUPPORT

Phoenix's policy of community support is one of the most valuable policies the company offers. In all its home office communities in Connecticut, Massachusetts, and New York, Phoenix encourages employees to share time, energy, and ideas with locally based programs and charities. The company supplements these volunteer efforts with financial contributions and social investments in local economic development and revitalization projects.

A prime example is its decade-old relationship with the Fred D. Wish School, a Hartford elementary school. Among other activities, students from the Wish School visit Phoenix's downtown office each week for one-on-one tutoring with company employees. The company also supports a number of other community institutions, such as the Greater Hartford Arts Council, University of Connecticut athletics, United Way, and Riverfront Recapture.

And, after serving as an official sponsor of the 1995 Special Olympics World Games, held in New Haven, Connecticut, Phoenix renewed its commitment to the Special Olympics movement by becoming the Title Sponsor of the Connecticut Special Olympics Unified Sports Program.

Phoenix is committed to bettering the economic and business environment of Hartford and all the communities where it does business. Progress is occurring step by step, by thoughtfully investing assets—finances and people power—in businesses and programs that contribute to long-term growth and prosperity.

Located near the banks of the Connecticut River in downtown Hartford, Phoenix's corporate offices (right) gained international attention in 1963 as the world's first two-sided building.

OXFORD HEALTH PLANS

Combine the best doctors with knowledgeable customer service representatives, flexible health-care plans, and innovative preventive-care programs, and the result will be Oxford Health Plans—the fastest-growing managed-care company in the nation—and about a million happy and healthy members in 1995. A young, energetic company with corporate headquarters in Norwalk, Connecticut, Oxford has offered customized health plans in the eastern U.S. since 1984.

Oxford's commitment to providing the very best health care begins with the very best doctors. All of Oxford's more than 20,000 participating physicians must meet extremely strict requirements, including being board-certified or recently board-eligible. By collaborating and communicating with doctors and by creating networks among physicians, Oxford enhances the ability of these top-notch medical professionals to provide the highest-quality, most cost-effective care.

In an effort to ensure the best personal service, highly skilled multilingual teams of customer service associates at Oxford's offices are thoroughly trained in all key areas so they can answer questions 24 hours a day, seven days a week. Such unusual service is one of the reasons Oxford Health Plans was rated number one for overall satisfaction among the leading managed-care plans in the metropolitan New York area on two recent independent consumer studies.

Designed to be flexible enough to meet the needs of large and small employers as well as the elderly and young families that require public assistance, Oxford's product lines include traditional HMOs, the point-of-service "Freedom Plan," third-party administration of employer-funded benefits, Medicare and Medicaid plans, and dental plans.

Knowing that prevention is the best medicine, Oxford has developed a number of innovative preventive programs. The "Healthy Mother, Healthy Baby" program provides expert care and counseling to pregnant members, while the "Better Breathing" program helps asthmatic members understand their condition and manage it more effectively. The "Active Partner" initiative advises members to schedule routine tests, childhood immunizations, and annual physicals.

Nationally, more and more local governments, businesses, and individuals are seeking the benefits that managed care offers. For Oxford, that means the opportunity for more exciting growth as a company while providing more customers with cost-effective, high-quality health care.

Stephen F. Wiggins founded Oxford Health Plans in 1984 with a vision to provide access to top-quality health care at affordable prices. Now, 1 million members and 3,700 employees later, Oxford is the fastest-growing employer in Connecticut and the fastest-growing managed-care firm in the United States.

HARTFORD HOSPITAL

Hartford Hospital, with its national reputation of excellence and innovation, is one of the largest and most sophisticated tertiary medical centers in the country. Located at 80 Seymour Street, on 70 acres within the South Green section of Hartford's center, the hospital has 940 beds, a free-standing physicians' office building, a free-standing data center, a cogeneration plant, six medical care walk-in centers, an independent medical laboratory, a cancer center, MRI facilities, and numerous indoor parking garages.

In 1980, Hartford Hospital was licensed for 1,025 beds and staffed 901 of those beds, employing 3,600 employees. Total admissions for 1980 were 38,000 inpatient and 160,000 combined emergency room and outpatient visits. Currently, the hospital is licensed for 940 beds. Employing 5,700 full- and part-time staff, Hartford Hospital is one of the city's largest employers of Hartford residents, and more than 30 percent of its employees reside in the city. The hospital's case load has grown to 180,000 E.R. and outpatient visits and 39,000 inpatients. Hartford Hospital receives 10 percent of all inpatient activity in Connecticut.

The affiliation between Veterans Memorial Medical Center, Hartford Hospital, and Newington Children's Hospital, forming the Connecticut Health System, makes Hartford Hospital an integral part of the largest health-care system in Connecticut. Coupled with the hospital's critical care helicopter service, LIFE STAR, Hartford Hospital is the premier specialty referral hospital in the north-central part of the state. As a Voluntary Hospital of America shareholder, Hartford Hospital has access to a wide variety of resources throughout the country.

Dynamic changes in the external environment as well as within its own neighborhood have challenged Hartford Hospital to develop innovative strategies as well as commit to widespread community programs aimed at assisting a minority population and refurbishing Hartford's South End. These programs have enabled the hospital to increase its market share when hospitals throughout the country are faced with fewer patients. Four distinct programs provide Hartford Hospital's major specialty focus: EMS/trauma, cardiac care, cancer care, and pediatrics. The hospital's national standing as a transplant center puts Hartford Hospital in the limelight with heart, kidney, pancreas, and liver procedures. Kidney transplantation has been performed at Hartford Hospital for over 20 years.

Other services include an ambulatory surgery center, a trauma center, an emergency center; a primary care unit; a cancer center; 20 outpatient clinics; full inpatient services; a 90-bed geriatric skilled nursing facility (located in Newington); an adult day-care center; the Kiwanis Pediatric Trauma Center; a radiation therapy oncology center; laboratories; home-care services; a foreign travel preventive medicine program; alcoholism counseling; allied health programs; 26 graduate educational programs in affiliation with the University of Connecticut School of Medicine and Dentistry; and a Health and Lifestyles program, which includes stress management, smoking cessation courses, and weight control and exercise seminars.

Hartford Hospital has been the recipient of numerous highly prestigious national awards, in recognition of its medical excellence as well as its work in the areas of minority recruitment and health services within the Hispanic community.

In the midst of major health-care reform nationally and persistent economic stress statewide, Saint Francis Hospital and Medical Center has remained constant in its commitment: to provide access to superb health care for every individual with great caring and at the lowest possible cost.

This commitment to caring includes providing all with whom the hospital comes in contact—from employees to patients to neighbors in Asylum and Blue Hills—with a sense of belonging, being understood, and appreciated regardless of race, gender, or physical or cultural differences. An appreciation for diversity is reflected in the mission given to Saint Francis by the founding Sisters of Saint Joseph of Chambery, an order committed to teaching and nursing the sick without regard for their religious creed, nationality, or beliefs.

Hailed as a "community triumph," the 1990 affiliation between Saint Francis and Mount Sinai Hospital benefits not only patients and their families, but the entire Greater Hartford region.

EXCELLENCE IN SEVERAL KEY AREAS

While most institutions claim just a few specialties, Saint Francis is a highly regarded leader in cardiology, oncology, trauma, rehabilitation, women's health, and mental health services. As part of a continuing commitment to Greater Hartford residents—and, indeed, to the entire region—Saint Francis has embarked on a labor of love, upgrading its facilities and technology.

Courtesy of Saint Francis Hospital and Medical Center

IMPORTANT NEW HEALTH-CARE FACILITIES FOR THE COMMUNITY

In the summer of 1996, a new patient-care facility is scheduled to open at Saint Francis. This addition to the Hartford skyline is part of a $114 million renovation project that began with the construction two years ago of the Saint Francis/Mount Sinai Regional Cancer Center. The 10-story building will accommodate expanded outpatient services, including, among other services, ambulatory surgery, critical care, and an attractive new women's pavilion.

In June 1995, Hartford's first medical rehabilitation hospital opened on the Mount Sinai campus. Care for traumatic brain injuries, which is linked with Saint Francis's Level I Trauma Center, is just one of the specialized programs offered by the 60-bed Rehabilitation Hospital of Connecticut.

This concern for improved health-care services is an expression of Saint Francis's continued commitment to Greater Hartford and to every member of the community.

For over 100 years, the Connecticut Institute for the Blind (CIB)/Oak Hill has been setting the standard in the quality of life available to people with visual impairments and multiple disabilities.

CIB/Oak Hill began in 1893, when Emily Wells Foster, a Sunday School teacher in Hartford, had a vision—to provide the means through which blind children could learn, grow, and lead meaningful, productive lives. Modestly, quietly, and with no financial support, she opened a nursery school with two blind boys as its first pupils.

For the next 18 years, blind children learned skills to foster their independence. In 1911, to meet the growing enrollment, Oak Hill School was built on Holcomb Street, and for the following 60 years, blind children received training in academic subjects, music, agriculture, athletics, and trades.

In the late 1970s, Lars Guldager became CIB/Oak Hill's executive director. At that time, with the passage of Public Law 94-142, blind children with no other significant disabilities were expected to attend public school with sighted children. Dr. Guldager laid the groundwork for CIB/Oak Hill to serve young people with visual impairment and other disabilities that ranged from mild to profound mental retardation. In 1976, CIB/Oak Hill enrolled its first students from the Department of Mental Retardation and opened its first group home in the community.

"Everyone has the right to live in his or her own community," says Dr. Guldager. "The concept of a small group home rather than an institution is based on a very traditional premise—the nuclear family. Our dedicated and caring staff are the family members who through encouragement and support help the residents reach their highest potential and become contributing members of their communities."

In the mid-1980s, a long-range plan was developed to address CIB/Oak Hill's philosophy that "isolated settings for living, working, and playing for any one homogeneous group is an unacceptable standard, damaging both to the individual members of the group and to the society in general." The goal of that plan was to have all CIB/Oak Hill residents integrated into Connecticut communities by 1995. In December 1995, that goal was met, as 368 residents were living in 64 group homes and 9 support living arrangements, working in 11 vocational sites, and learning in 5 classrooms in 41 Connecticut towns. CIB/Oak Hill's staff of close to 1,000 people provide the administrative and direct-care support that helps people with multiple disabilities participate fully in their communities.

CIB/Oak Hill also offers respite services for children and adults with multiple disabilities, providing them the opportunity to experience CIB/Oak Hill's programs while briefly living away from home; summer camp for people with multiple disabilities, enabling them to enjoy such activities as swimming, boating, horseback riding, and trips; computer camp for blind and visually impaired students, combining summer camp activities with computer instruction; the Ella Anderson Resource Room, designed to meet the information needs of people with visual impairments, including text-to-braille

production, computer training, and adaptive equipment consulting; workshops for the community and schools on disabilities awareness; and equipment adaptations to make life easier and more enjoyable for people with severe physical disabilities.

Future plans for CIB/Oak Hill include making existing programs available to more people and expanding its supported living program, which enables people with disabilities to live independently. Plans are under way to develop The Hartford Artisans' Center, a collaborative program among CIB/Oak Hill, OPUS/Arts and the Aging, and the City of Hartford's Elderly Services Division. The center will provide people with disabilities and the elderly with supplemental income and opportunities to socialize through the creation of high-quality crafts. CIB/Oak Hill is also studying the demand for a health club and sports center accessible to people

with disabilities and is developing new programs for underserved people with disabilities, such as a teen club and an extended learning program for people who are blind or visually impaired.

Some of these programs have already been implemented; others are in the exploratory or planning stages. According to Chairman of the Board John J. Dwyer, "All will be characterized

with the same outstanding performance for which CIB/Oak Hill has been recognized."

The quality on which CIB/Oak Hill has built its reputation can best be summed up by Marcel, a CIB/Oak Hill resident who came to CIB/Oak Hill from an institution: "This place is much better. Here, they're nice to me. Here, they listen."

Hospital for Special Care is a private, not-for-profit rehabilitation and chronic disease hospital located in New Britain, Connecticut.

Guided by its 50-year heritage, Hospital for Special Care helps patients achieve lasting improvements in the quality of their lives through a variety of inpatient and outpatient programs. These programs fall into three distinct service lines: rehabilitation, respiratory care, and pediatrics.

The rehabilitation service line provides intensive inpatient and outpatient programs for people recovering from stroke, pulmonary disease, head injury, orthopedic conditions, neurological diseases, or long-term illnesses. The respiratory care service line provides individualized treatment for patients with respiratory problems and those requiring ventilator or oxygen support. The hospital's pediatric service line cares for children with special long-term medical needs.

The goal of each service line team is

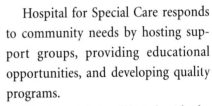

to consistently provide high-quality care not only to improve health but to improve the quality of life for each patient. Doctors, nurses, therapists, and other staff work together, helping patients return to more productive lives.

This emphasis on teamwork and communication, combined with sophisticated technologies and fully modernized facilities, enables the hospital to provide a continuum of care from admission through discharge and beyond.

Hospital for Special Care responds to community needs by hosting support groups, providing educational opportunities, and developing quality programs.

The hospital is affiliated with the University of Connecticut as a teaching facility. It is also accredited by the Joint Commission on Accreditation of Healthcare Organizations (JCAHO) and the Commission on Accreditation of Rehabilitation Facilities (CARF).

Reaching beyond its campus, Hospital for Special Care shares its expertise with local community and professional groups by providing free speakers bureau lectures. Connecticut's school nurses also benefit by receiving hands-on training in caring for medically complex children who are mainstreamed into public classrooms.

Each of these efforts reinforces the hospital's values–caring, integrity, and the pursuit of excellence–and makes Hospital for Special Care Connecticut's rehabilitation expert.

Connecticut Children's Medical Center resulted from a strategic alliance involving Newington Children's Hospital, Hartford Hospital, and the University of Connecticut Health Center. Opening in 1996, it will be Connecticut's leading freestanding pediatric hospital.

The 138-bed facility consolidates all primary, acute, and tertiary pediatric services previously offered separately at Newington Children's, Hartford, and UConn's John Dempsey hospitals. The pediatric program for the university's medical school will also be housed there.

A wide range of medical and social outreach programs for children and families will be based at the center, improving the community's quality of life through health-care education and pediatric preventive care. Even before opening, the new medical center endowed the Children's Fund of Connecticut with more than $15 million to support innovative programs in such areas as the prevention and treatment of lead poisoning and children's mental health problems.

Located at 282 Washington Street, near downtown Hartford, the medical center was designed by the prominent Dallas-based architectural firm of HKS, Inc., which has designed 30 other children's hospitals nationally. Connecticut Children's Medical Center was constructed with the special needs of children in mind. Created with community involvement, its interior design incorporates the themes of science, toys, and home, and all of the building's art was collected from the community, including children's art gathered from all over Connecticut.

The medical center will also have a significant economic impact on Hartford. Directly employing more than 600 people, it is expected to support 700 more jobs in and around the city. It also will directly stimulate the annual purchase of $25.8 million in goods and services from Hartford businesses. Finally, the City of Hartford will benefit from more than $1 million annually in new payments in lieu of property taxes.

Beyond that, Connecticut Children's Medical Center is expected to attract top pediatricians and medical researchers to the Hartford area, directly affecting the quality of life and helping to attract research dollars and biomedical and pharmaceutical companies to Hartford.

In combination, for all of these reasons, Connecticut children will surely be healthier because of the new Connecticut Children's Medical Center.

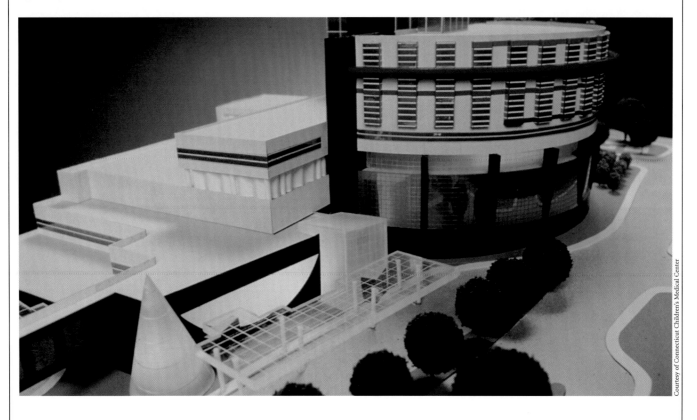

Courtesy of Connecticut Children's Medical Center

Founded in 1822 at the dawn of the humanitarian movement in mental health care, The Institute of Living was the first hospital of any kind in Connecticut and the second psychiatric hospital in the United States. Early on, The Institute's doctors, nurses, and administrators dedicated themselves to providing every patient with high-quality care in an atmosphere of compassion and respect.

Never wavering from that philosophy, the Hartford Retreat (as it was then known) gained national prominence in the 1930s and '40s as a haven for wealthy celebrities and Hollywood legends. Today, The Institute has moved far from that era and into the mainstream of medical science, offering hope to the people most in need.

As Hartford Hospital's Mental Health Network, The Institute of Living provides a full spectrum of behavioral health and addiction recovery services to people of all ages. Recent affiliation with one of the state's largest acute care hospitals allows access to specialty services in a variety of areas and a continuum of care unmatched in the state.

Depending upon the unique needs of the patients, The Institute offers consultation services; outpatient services; partial hospital day programs; residential programs in supervised apartments; inpatient programs; and crisis intervention. A new and unique centralized assessment center functions as both entry point and immediate care center.

New treatment techniques, new generations of psychopharmacological therapies, and access to cutting-edge technology mean quicker diagnosis and a briefer length of treatment than ever before. Emphasis is placed on treating the patient effectively and efficiently, with the least disruption to home and work life possible. Most of The Institute's patients continue to live at home or in the nearby community during treatment.

Specialty services also enable patients to receive the care they need with others experiencing similar problems. Programs focused on eating disorders, geriatric issues, addiction recovery, child and adolescent problems, and professionals' needs offer specific care for specific problems. A school for elementary, middle, and high school students enables young people to receive an education and therapy simultaneously.

Part of a collaborative network of mental health professionals throughout Connecticut, The Institute provides services well beyond Greater Hartford.

The Donnelly Building at The Institute of Living

Situated on a strikingly beautiful 150-acre suburban campus in Farmington, only eight miles from Hartford, the University of Connecticut Health Center's modern 10-story complex dominates the skyline as one approaches exit 39 traveling east on I-84. This imposing modern building houses many of the state-of-the-art teaching, research, and patient-care activities of the university's nationally acclaimed schools of medicine and dental medicine.

The Health Center's faculty utilize its 232-bed John Dempsey Hospital and Kevin V. Dowling medical office complex to provide specialized and routine inpatient and outpatient care. These modern health-care facilities are major sites for primary care and serve as specialized medical referral centers for patients from the greater Hartford region as well as the rest of Connecticut, New England, and the nation. The campus is home to several nationally recognized clinical centers, including the Multidisciplinary Arthritis Center, the Connecticut Chemosensory Center, the Alcohol and Drug Treatment Center, and the Travelers Center on Aging, as well as several regionally unique and outstanding programs, such as the neonatal intensive care unit, the Jean Marie Colbert Bone Marrow Transplant Center, the Kidney Stone Center, and the Connecticut Cancer Institute. In addition to all that happens on its Farmington campus, the Health Center provides a wide variety of health-care services and educational programs in Hartford and communities across the state.

The Health Center is Connecticut's only publicly supported academic health center and receives about 19 percent of its annual operating budget of over $300 million from the state's General Fund and student tuition. The remainder of its revenues comes from patient-care services (more than $200 million), federal, industrial, and foundation research grants and contracts (over $40 million), philanthropic support, and other non-state sources.

The Health Center's primary mission is "education at the undergraduate, graduate, and professional level for practitioners, teachers, and researchers." The facilities in Farmington are characterized by an environment of exemplary care, excellence in research, and a commitment to public service that provides the educational milieu for some of the finest students in the country.

Approximately 320 "undergraduates" work toward their M.D. degree in the School of Medicine and about 160 toward their D.M.D. degree in the School of Dental Medicine. The schools take pride in the high caliber and diverse composition of their students. Women represent 50 percent of the student body, and 18 percent of the students come from underrepresented minority groups. Through a variety of residency programs, the schools provide and coordinate the postgraduate education of more than 500 graduate physicians and dentists each year. In addition, nursing and allied health professions students train in the Health Center's clinical facilities as well as those of their affiliated institutions. The Health Center also offers programs leading to the Ph.D. degree in the

Centrally located. From its suburban location eight miles west of Hartford and just a few minutes' drive from the intersection of I-84 and Route 9, the UConn Health Center provides a wide range of inpatient and outpatient services, including an emergency department staffed 24 hours a day by board-certified physicians, as well as diverse programs in biomedical education and research.

biomedical sciences (100 students) and the master's degree in public health (220 students). Approximately 25 percent of the Ph.D. candidates concurrently pursue their M.D. degree.

The Health Center faculty provides many courses and lectures for practicing health-care professionals and the public at large. These programs range from nationally recognized continuing medical education classes for professionals to lectures for high school and other school-aged students to the renowned "mini-medical school," which advances the public's knowledge of health and health care.

The Health Center faculty do some of the most advanced research in the country. The faculty are members of the National Academy of Science and recipients of prestigious Claude Pepper Fellowships and Kellogg Foundation Scholar designations and are awarded many millions of dollars in highly competitive, peer-reviewed research grants from the National Institutes of Health,

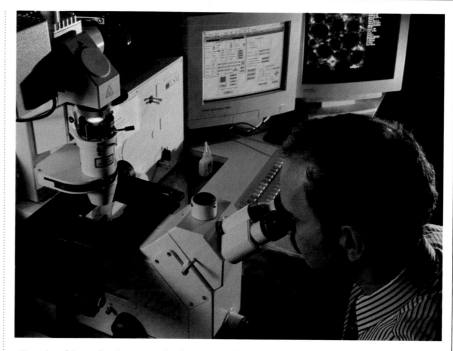

Creating biomedical images. Leslie Loew, Ph.D., director of the Center for Biomedical Imaging Technology, uses a technically specialized confocal microscope to create a detailed image of lung tissue. In addition to supporting research by scientists at the Health Center, the Imaging Center is used extensively by investigators at corporations like Pfizer and Miles.

the National Science Foundation, more than 50 national and international industry and business organizations, and many of the nation's most distinguished foundations, associations, councils, and societies.

The Health Center has a strong, long-standing commitment to developing the intellectual properties conceived in its laboratories into products to improve the health and quality of life of the public. Each year Health Center faculty make numerous scientific discoveries that often lead to patents that, in turn, are transferred to the public domain, resulting

Remarkable care. UConn Health Center's continuum of care includes primary care, prevention and rehabilitation services, acute medical care, and selected, highly specialized care for serious illnesses and injuries. Many of these programs serve as educational venues for medical students and residents, such as Jill Banatoski, class of 1995.

in the creation of licensing agreements with many of the country's leading pharmaceutical companies. Several of these technologies have resulted in the development of new startup companies. In addition, the Health Center's federally funded General Clinical Research Center (one of only 75 in the nation) is a site for the study of many of the newest and most promising clinical technologies and pharmaceuticals available. Thus, should they be stricken with a difficult or particularly threatening disease, patients at the Health Center have the opportunity to take advantage of the most advanced therapies available.

Whether it is educating the next generation of health-care practitioners and scientists, creating knowledge that advances science and medicine, or providing the highest-quality care in a personal yet cost-effective way, the University of Connecticut Health Center is dedicated to innovation and excellence.

Managing a world of opportunities. That's what Loctite Corporation is all about," says David Freeman, Loctite's president and chief executive officer. "Anyone who assembles, manufactures, repairs, or maintains things is a potential Loctite customer. And because we do business all over the world, Loctite literally has a world of opportunities. By capitalizing on these opportunities, we grow and prosper."

That philosophy certainly seems to work well for this international specialty chemicals company. Loctite has grown and prospered significantly since its birth in 1953 in Professor Vernon Krieble's chemistry lab at Trinity College in Hartford. Sales have increased nearly 300 percent in the past 10 years alone, from $240 million to more than $800 million. Profits have shown an even more impressive increase, from $20 million to nearly

Loctite Corporation strives to be a leader in the development of new products for the markets it serves. In addition, innovations in the area of convenience packaging have been enthusiastically received by consumers.

$100 million. The company now does business in 80 countries and has direct subsidiaries in 40.

INNOVATIVE SOLUTIONS

Innovation is the driving force behind Loctite's growth. While many companies focus on their competition, Loctite focuses on its customers and the marketplace. "Our goal is to find new and improved solutions to our customers' problems," says Freeman.

A HISTORY OF RESEARCH AND DEVELOPMENT

With missionary zeal, company founder Krieble and his son, Bob, experimented in the early 1950s with a liquid adhesive called tetraethylene glycol dimethacrylate. In those days, no one knew what to do with this strange substance that hardened in the absence of oxygen. Few recognized its potential, and no one had discovered a way to keep the compound in its liquid state for easy storage.

But the Kriebles persisted, and soon they discovered that they could preserve the compound in polyethylene bottles. That discovery led to the first commercial product of the fledgling family enterprise—then called the American Sealants Company.

When Bob's wife, Nancy, suggested the company be called Loctite, it stuck as fast as the company's new glue. The Loctite trademark was registered, and in 1959—six years after his initial discovery—Krieble earned his first patent. By 1961, annual sales had reached $1 million.

Since then, growth has been rapid, with the company's fortunes buoyed by

an ever-increasing array of new products and a campaign to acquire promising companies. But success has not led to complacency; the vision and commitment to experimentation so characteristic of the company's founder remain its lifeblood.

"Loctite was started in a laboratory," says Freeman, "and research and development continue to be the key to our success. In the past three years, we've invested almost $80 million in creating new products and finding new methods for our customers." More than 25 percent of Loctite's nearly 1,000 products were developed in the past five years, and the number of new product offerings is constantly increasing.

'HOMETOWN' FLAVOR, GLOBAL RENOWN

Throughout its history, Loctite has remained a Hartford company. From its original headquarters in Newington to its current corporate headquarters in Hartford Square North and its recently completed North American Group headquarters in Rocky Hill, Loctite has embodied Connecticut's famed Yankee ingenuity.

Yet the company's borders extend far beyond Connecticut. Loctite is a truly global corporation. In fact, Loctite crossed the Atlantic before crossing the Mississippi. Loctite opened distributorships in France and the United Kingdom in 1957; and within just six years of its founding, foreign sales accounted for one-fourth of the company's volume.

Today, approximately 60 percent of Loctite's business comes from overseas sales. Loctite's specialty sealants, adhesives, and coatings are basic ingredients in industrial and automotive markets throughout the world. Virtually every industry, from paper mills to producers of hypodermic needles, relies on Loctite somewhere along its production line.

And because the company's market diversity mirrors its product diversity, Loctite has survived the economic downturns that have sent other New England manufacturers into a tailspin. "Because we operate globally, there is no single client that accounts for more than one percent of our business," says Freeman. "Therefore, we're far less affected than other companies by fluctuations in any one industry."

Universal Appeal and Application

Just as Loctite's products have worldwide distribution, so, too, do they have universal appeal and application. Fine art, crystal, and watches are repaired with a Loctite bond. The plastic eyes on a child's teddy bear are attached with Loctite glue. Automobile air-bag restraints use Loctite's NUVA-SIL® products to speed up the production process. And repairs on everything from model trains to racers at the Indy 500 are made with Loctite adhesives.

In addition, some dramatic new Loctite products are being tested: medical adhesives to close incisions, electrically conductive adhesives, heat-resistant adhesives, and more. Loctite enjoys uncontested dominance in many consumer markets as well. Such familiar Loctite products as Quicktite® SuperGlue are used by consumers throughout the world. In fact, hobbyists and do-it-yourselfers account for millions in sales each year, making Loctite the world's largest producer of such products.

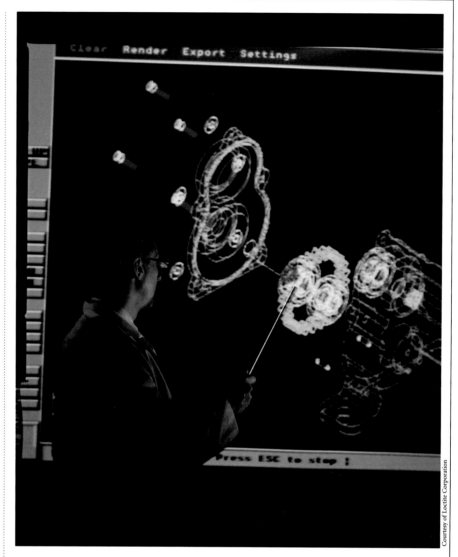

Spearheading the use of advanced design engineering methods, Loctite Corporation works with suppliers and customers to find better ways to solve customers' needs.

Loctite recently patented a new consumer product, Houseworks™ Microwave Energized Glue, which, after being heated for a few minutes in a household microwave oven, bonds almost any surface. Because it then returns to a solid state, the glue can't ever dry up, so it's reusable with virtually no waste.

As the company's president and CEO, Freeman brings both international and domestic expertise to the company. He joined Loctite in 1974 as financial director of Loctite U.K., then advanced to vice president of the Loctite European Group in 1979. In 1981, he came to the U.S. as vice president of finance of Loctite International. He was named chief financial officer in 1983, president of the North American Group in 1985, and executive vice president, chief operating officer, and member of the Loctite Board of Directors in 1990. He became president in 1991 and added chief executive officer responsibilities in 1993.

"Loctite's story contains an important message for other companies in the state," says Freeman. "Make wise use of your local resources, but keep your sights global. There's a world of opportunities for companies with that vision."

Started as a small family business at the turn of the century, The Wiremold Company has grown into the world's leading maker of wire management systems for power, voice, data, video, and cable distribution.

D. Hayes Murphy began the business in 1900 when he purchased the Richmond Electric Conduit Company. In 1916, the first products with the Wiremold® name were sold. The 500 Metal Raceway, a pioneer Wiremold product, is still on the market today in its original configuration. In 1926, the business became known as The Wiremold Company. Milwaukee, Pittsburgh, and Hartford were all home to the company until 1929, when it established headquarters in West Hartford, Connecticut.

Access™ 5000 Raceway is the first product to combine the practical advantages of raceway technology with a designer look that blends attractively into any office environment.

Wiremold products are shaping the way buildings are designed and constructed. In modern office environments where people move almost as fast as technology, there is a need for fast, easy access to power, phone, and computer lines. Traditional "behind the wall" wiring systems are becoming obsolete since they require expensive and intrusive retrofitting for every addition or change to the wiring scheme. In contrast, Wiremold wire management systems are modular, accessible, and expandable, saving hours of labor time and thousands of dollars for cost-conscious building owners and operators.

With the most comprehensive set of wire management solutions on the market, including innovative new products like Access™ 5000 Raceway, Wiremold systems are fast becoming "the only way to wire." Wiremold is also a leading supplier of power conditioning and surge protection systems to protect vital equipment.

The company's current reputation stems not only from the products it makes, but the way that it makes them. Two thousand employees have worked to give Wiremold a worldwide reputation for manufacturing excellence through its Kaizen approach. Top manufacturing companies from throughout the U.S. and the world have visited the Wiremold West Hartford plant to observe Kaizen (Japanese for "continuous improvement") in action.

CEO magazine and *Target*, the magazine for manufacturing excellence, have recognized Wiremold for its model approach to cycle time

The 500 Metal Raceway, a pioneer Wiremold product, is still on the market today in its original configuration.

improvement and just-in-time production. And Wiremold executives have been featured speakers at numerous conferences, including the MIT-sponsored Manufacturing Leadership Summit at Harvard.

The company is now experiencing the healthiest growth in its history as it continues to develop new products to meet the growing demand for wire management solutions. A series of acquisitions through the early and mid-1990s, including **Walker Systems, Inc.,** of Parkersburg, West Virginia, in 1993, **Interlink Technologies** of Broomall, Pennsylvania, in 1995, and **Raceway Components, Inc.,** of Paterson, New Jersey, in 1995, also have fueled company growth.

The prospects for continued expansion look promising through the year 2000 as The Wiremold Company continues to set the pace for excellence in the design and manufacture of wire management systems, power conditioning, and surge suppression products.

P/A Industries

Metal latches on suitcases, eyeglass frames, venetian blinds. What do all of these extremely useful items found in millions of households have in common? All are made with the assistance of press-feeding and coil-handling equipment technology from P/A Industries, Inc., of Bloomfield. Since 1954, P/A has manufactured automation equipment for the metal-stamping industry, including electronic servo roll feeds, air feeds, stock straighteners, stock reels, scrap choppers, and transporters.

Thanks to the precision and high quality of its products, P/A is a supplier to such manufacturing giants as GE, Stanley, Gillette, Samsonite, and Hamilton Beach. P/A's innovative designs are user-friendly and engineered to keep productivity up by optimizing press speeds, feed accuracy, and set-up times. Each machine is assembled, built, and tested in P/A's fully equipped 60,000-square-foot facility just north of Hartford.

Committed to Connecticut and the importance of keeping stable manufacturing industries in the region, P/A is considered a world leader in its field and has sold its equipment in 38 countries. Within the last several years, P/A's export-minded management has established several strategic offshore operations: P/A Retain Ltd, Taiwan; P/A Bohemia SRO, Czech Republic; P/A Mectool AB, Sweden; and P/A GmbH, Germany.

While the bulk of P/A's sales fall into the category of coil-feeding and handling equipment, the company responds to the needs of its customers, developing and redefining systems that require special engineering and custom designs. P/A also keeps abreast of the latest innovations in the industry and continuously updates its cutting-edge CAD technology.

Growth for the company has been astonishing—in double digits since the beginning of the 1990s—proving that the conservatively managed 50 plus-person organization has a solid foundation. With engineers who have been credited with more patents than those of any other company in their field and with sales and administrative staff who with decades of experience are motivated to increase growth, year after year, P/A Industries believes its future holds great promise and includes an expanded workforce in Connecticut.

HEUBLEIN INC.

For more than a century, the words Heublein and Hartford have been inseparable, nearly synonymous—although the name did cause some difficulty for the good people of Hartford at first. A most peculiar name, they thought. How do you pronounce it? Hyblein? Hew-blein? Hooblein? Hoi-blein?

It was too much for the citizens of Hartford. But they all agreed that the choice foods and beverages served at The Heublein were out of this world. The small hotel and cafe that Andrew Heublein started on lower Mulberry Street in 1859 became a popular gathering spot for businessmen, visiting celebrities, theater folk playing Hartford, and political notables.

In 1875, Herr Heublein relinquished the business to sons Gilbert and Louis, who expanded as "bottlers and whole-sale wine dealers."

One of the reasons for the gaiety in the gay '90s was the cocktail—a symbol of sophisticated sociability. The serendipitous discovery of premixed cocktails by Heublein led to Hartford becoming home to the world-famous Club Cocktails.

The business was incorporated as G.F. Heublein & Brother in 1901, and the company invaded state after state with its specialties, growing in reputation for the highest standard of quality. The tradition grew internationally as well, as the brothers blossomed out as exporters, with branch offices in New York, Frankfurt, Germany, and London.

Prohibition interrupted the business from 1919 through 1933. But A-1 Sauce, acquired by Heublein in 1906, kept the Hartford home fires burning until Heublein's wines and spirits could make their thirstily awaited comeback. With the repeal of prohibition, the Heubleins reentered the liquor business with their well-known specialties.

In 1939, Gilbert Heublein's grandson, John G. Martin, launched the modern company when he purchased the rights to manufacture a totally unknown Russian spirit. Spurred by the genius of Martin, Hartford became home to the social and marketing revolution that introduced America to the virtues of Smirnoff Vodka—and changed the drinking habits of the country.

John Martin continued to shape the company's future for the next three decades, and Heublein remained a family-owned business until it went public in 1959.

During the 1960s, the company acquired many additional brands of wines and spirits and built production facilities in Michigan and California. Among Heublein's acquisitions were the Arrow Liqueurs Company in 1964, International Vintage Wines (importers of Lancers Rose) in 1965, and the U.S. agency for Jose Cuervo Tequila in 1966. The company expanded into the rapidly growing California wine industry in 1969, purchasing Beaulieu Vineyard in the Napa Valley. Smirnoff Vodka, on its way to becoming the most popular brand of spirits in the U.S., grew to become an international favorite as well during the '60s.

By 1970, Heublein had become the marketing leader in the industry and recognized as one of the top marketing companies in the U.S., with production facilities in 34 countries and sales of its food, wine, and spirits products in more than 100 markets.

In 1982, when Heublein had become a $1 billion business, the company merged with R.J. Reynolds, one of the largest corporations in America. In 1987, the company was acquired by Grand Metropolitan PLC of London. In this new role, Heublein became the anchor of International Distillers and Vintners' North American operations, which included Paddington Corporation, Carillon Importers, Gilbey-Canada, and a joint venture in Mexico.

Since then, Heublein has continued to expand its product line through the development and acquisition of new brands, including T.G.I. Friday's Cocktails, Christian Brothers Brandy, and Glen Ellen wines. Its John G. Martin Technical Center, located on New Park Avenue in Hartford, is a tribute to the innovation of its modern-day founding father. The center consists of 30,000 square feet of laboratory and administrative space and a state-of-the-art 10,000-square-foot Technical Operations Laboratory, where the company continues its tradition of product innovation.

The multibillion-dollar Heublein of today bears little resemblance to the family-owned business of Hartford. But anchored in the city of its birth, the company continues in the spirit of generations of people whose inspiration, imagination, and dedication fueled a philosophy and a business that has far surpassed the dreams of its founders.

Liz Ozog, a chemist in Heublein's Research and Development Department in Hartford

The Residence Inn by Marriott, located just minutes north of Hartford at 100 Dunfey Lane in Windsor, features the finest in all-suites lodging. The inn offers a full range of conveniences that appeal to business travelers, leisure travelers, and families—especially guests planning to stay longer than just a few days.

In the past, travelers away from home for an extended time had to use traditional hotels. Residence Inn by Marriott is designed specifically with those travelers in mind. The warm, homelike surroundings make Residence Inn truly unique.

With spacious sleeping and living areas and a full-size, fully equipped kitchen, the Residence Inn's spacious suites are nearly 50 percent larger than conventional hotel rooms.

Two floor plans are available—studio and two-story penthouse suites. Both provide plenty of room for guests to work, entertain, and unwind. Most suites offer a cozy wood-burning fireplace. The spectacular penthouse suites offer endless versatility for two people or a family. Each has two bedroom areas, two full bathrooms, two closets, even two televisions.

Residence Inn provides a unique range of special complimentary services—a fitness center, a pool, happy-hour social events, and an extensive breakfast buffet—to make the stay more relaxing. Staff will even do grocery shopping for guests at no additional charge.

Marriott's reputation for excellence in hospitality and service means its staff is dedicated to making sure every

Courtesy of Residence Inn

guest has the most memorable and satisfying stay possible. For many years the name Marriott has been associated with the finest in hospitality. At Residence Inn, everyone strives to ensure that both the facilities and services live up to that reputation.

SIMSCROFT-ECHO FARMS

Since its founding as a dairy farm in 1941, Simscroft-Echo Farms has literally and figuratively played a constructive role in the development of the Farmington River Valley and the rest of Connecticut.

The Simsbury-based company has grown rapidly from its agrarian origins. In the 1960s, Lionel Girard, the founder, and his brother, Dominique, began transforming the company from an agricultural business into a construction firm, and it soon underwent rapid growth. Their first project involved developing their farmland into a residential subdivision.

Today, Simscroft-Echo Farms, Inc., is a major general site contractor and subcontractor, providing a range of services for its customers. The company specializes in site excavation and road and utility construction, but it offers commercial snow-removal service, street and parking lot sweeping, and building demolition as well.

Lionel Girard retired in 1972—the year the company was incorporated—and handed the reins over to his sons Michael and David and a nephew, Daniel. In 1975, another Girard brother, Greg, became a partner in the company.

The Girard brothers brought to the business the same sense of commitment and vision their father had. Through the 1970s, the company continued to expand in the residential construction market. In 1978, the Girards added a gravel-pit operation, with locations in Simsbury and Granby. In the 1980s, the company focused on commercial and industrial construction and again experienced growth while adding another operation, Simscroft Sweeping Services, Inc., to complement the construction company.

Simscroft-Echo Farms, Inc., and its affiliated companies continue to prosper. The company employs more than 100 people and has a modern fleet of more than 130 trucks and related construction equipment.

In 1994, Michael Girard won the Greater Hartford Chamber of Commerce "Mid-Size Business Leader of the Year" Award. And in 1995, Simscroft-Echo Farms earned first place in the University of Connecticut's NOZKO Family Business Leadership Awards in the mid-size business category.

With a strong base of private commercial and industrial customers and an expanding market of public utility and road construction projects, this family-owned and managed company remains committed to its primary mission: providing competitively priced, timely, and well-managed construction projects for customers throughout Connecticut.

Left to right: Daniel, Greg, David, and Mike Girard

HOLIDAY INN HARTFORD-DOWNTOWN

It's been said that the measure of a city's hospitality is ultimately determined by the comfort and relaxation one achieves during one's lodging experience. We're creatures of comfort, and the Holiday Inn Hartford-Downtown knows how to ensure that the need for comfort is met.

From the moment one steps into its richly appointed lobby or dines in its gracious restaurant, one knows one has made the right choice for one's evening stay, dining experience, or special event.

Located in the heart of Connecticut, the full-service Holiday Inn Hartford-Downtown combines luxurious but affordable accommodations with easy access for the business or recreational traveler. And for those looking to celebrate

a special occasion, superb catering and expert preplanning and coordination will ensure success.

The 18-floor hotel overlooking the scenic Connecticut River offers 342 rooms, one-bedroom suites, and an executive level. These spacious rooms feature remote-control cable television with in-room movies on Command Video, clock radios, and large desks. Guests can choose from deluxe two-bed accommodations, king-size bedrooms, or elegant two-room suites. Rooms for nonsmoking and disabled guests are also available. An elegantly appointed, versatile meeting space includes conference rooms and banquet facilities designed to accommodate from 10 to 350 people.

"Our goal is to offer casual and business travelers a 'one-stop hospitality' center, whether they are visiting Hartford for one evening, for an afternoon business function, or for weeks," says General Manager Karen Sikora-Berard. "Our meeting and conference facilities offer every convenience, including a fully equipped business-support center. We offer a complete fitness center with a stair master, life cycle, treadmill, weight machines, and an outdoor pool.

"We're known for our variety of special amenities," she adds, "and you can't beat the location—just minutes from Bradley International Airport, three minutes from the train and bus station, and literally minutes from all downtown activities. And we'll help you get here from the airport or deliver you to most of your chosen doorsteps. We are the only hotel in downtown Hartford that offers complimentary shuttle service."

The Holiday Inn Hartford-Downtown is within easy walking distance of everything Connecticut's capital city has to offer: colorful shops, wonderful restaurants, historic sites and museums, and the Hartford Civic Center, with three levels of exciting shops, restaurants, conference facilities, and an 18,000-seat arena, home to the Hartford Whalers, Meadows Music Theater, and a variety of shows and concerts.

If you're looking for an evening on the town, the Hartford Stage Company, Theaterworks, and the rest of Hartford's Arts and Entertainment District are close by. So are the Wadsworth Atheneum, Hartford's world-class art museum; Bushnell Memorial Hall; the Old State House; the Mark Twain House; and the state capitol.

For business travelers, the Holiday Inn Hartford-Downtown is close to federal and state government offices; several large insurance companies, including Aetna Life and Casualty, Travelers, Phoenix, Hartford Steam Boiler, ITT Hartford, and CIGNA; United Technologies corporate headquarters and Pratt & Whitney Aircraft; and state and technical colleges, the University of Connecticut, the University of Hartford, and the Hartford Graduate Center.

Within an hour's drive are the Foxwoods High Stakes Bingo and Casino, historic Sturbridge Village, the Essex steam train and riverboat, Mystic Seaport Museum and Aquarium, the beach, and dozens of other exciting tourist activities.

BRADLEY INTERNATIONAL AIRPORT & SIGNATURE FLIGHT SUPPORT

Bradley International Airport has become one of New England's largest major airports. Located north of Hartford, Connecticut, Bradley International provides both leisure and business travelers throughout western New England with easy access to any major city or vacation spot.

With 20 carriers offering over 275 flights to and from 75 destinations every day, Bradley International is the most convenient alternative to the congested city airports of New York or Boston. That means fewer delays at the airport, less time fighting traffic, and more time enjoying your trip.

In addition to efficient scheduled service, Bradley has become a more frequently used cargo alternative in the Northeast. Unencumbered by tunnels, bridges, or tolls and with virtually no congestion on regional highways, Bradley has freight services that are a cost-effective option when moving import and export material.

Bradley International Airport

Bradley International is currently served by Signature Flight Support, one of two fixed-base operators at the airport. Signature Flight Support is Bradley's recent addition to the airport. Covering 22 acres, Signature Hartford is one of 36 Signature facilities across the United States and serves as the flagship facility in the Signature Flight Support network. Its two-story structure houses 17,000 square feet of executive terminal and office space, 22,000 square feet of transient hangar space, and 50,000 square feet of hangar and office space that serves Signature's premier client, United Technologies.

Sensitive to the needs of the corporate passenger and crew, Signature Hartford has spared no expense with glass telephone booths, which are complete with a data port and desk; the state-of-the-art WSI/DUAT flight-planning station; the private shower facilities; or the large pilot lounging area, equipped with the latest in satellite technology and, of course, Signature's famous complimentary Saturn crew cars and Cannondale mountain bikes.

Signature Hartford has a full technical services department with maintenance capabilities for Gulfstream III and IV, Hawker 1000, Citation Ultra, and the S-76 helicopter. This department offers aviation restoration services, including cleaning and interior work on the aircraft. Signature also offers a cargo handling and warehousing department on the east side of Bradley International Airport.

Courtesy of Signature Flight Support

Helping people in need was the top priority when the late Harvey Kagan founded Professional Ambulance Service in 1963 by investing $500 in his first ambulance. Back then, ambulances were low-ceilinged Cadillacs that didn't provide much room for treating the patient. Basic first aid was the limit of care.

Today, more than 30 years later, the company Harvey Kagan founded receives all the 911 calls in Hartford and West Hartford and responds with highly trained medical professionals in vehicles furnished with a host of high-tech equipment. Things have certainly changed.

The Professional Group, as it is now known, provides not only emergency medical care in ambulances but also nonemergency medical transportation for more than 600 people each day. Consisting of Professional Ambulance Service, Professional Wheelchair Transportation, L & M Ambulance Corporation, Trinity Ambulance Service, and Maple Hill Ambulance, the

Courtesy of Professional Group

Professional Group has 31 ambulances, 21 wheelchair-lift vans, 14 medical livery sedans, as well as limousines and supply vehicles. Three hundred and fifty employees work at the 22,000-square-foot headquarters in West Hartford and at several satellite offices.

While the expansion of the company is due in large part to the desire of Harvey Kagan and his partner, Morton Appleton, who is now the company's president, to be the biggest and best

ambulance service around, the company's strategy of diversification was also a means of meeting the changing transportation needs of the community. People didn't just need emergency ambulance rides to the hospital. They also needed nonemergency transportation to hospitals and doctors' offices, as well as special medical transportation to other parts of New England and the country.

The staff of the Professional Group reflects the company's desire to be progressive and to provide full service. Certified paramedics and emergency medical technicians, who have hundreds of hours of training and continuing education, provide a range of services from advanced cardiac life support to IVs, intubations, and other procedures. The company has always put the patient first, and this is reflected in the expertise of its medical professionals, who receive regular in-house training, in partnership with the city's hospitals, and participate in the research and development of new equipment and procedures.

Providing the crucial link to the "road crews," the Professional Group's dispatchers use a high-tech vehicle-tracking system that enables them to pinpoint the location of an ambulance within 50 feet. Certified mechanics are on staff to keep the fleet of vehicles in top condition. Professional administrative and management staff keep abreast of the latest developments in the health-care field and form networks with hospitals, insurance companies, and managed-care providers.

From its earliest days, the Professional Group maintained a strong commitment to the community. It was the first ambulance company in Connecticut to form partnerships with volunteer ambulance corps in Hartford's suburbs, lending vehicles and providing trained staff to ensure coverage 24 hours a day. Today, the Professional Group continues to pioneer programs that help people in outlying areas reach the city's hospitals quickly and safely.

Educational outreach is an important part of the company's commitment. By working with educational institutions in New England, the Professional Group offers learning opportunities for paramedics and emergency medical technicians (EMTs) in training. Recently, the Professional Group received the New Hampshire Technical Institute Paramedic Service Award. The Professional Group is also a training facility for American Heart Association CPR courses, through which more than 2,000 community members are trained annually. Teaming up with local school systems, the company's ambulance crews educate schoolchildren about using 911 and emergency services.

The company also provides more than 400 hours of community service in the form of ambulance coverage at community youth sports events and at road races that raise money for charity. In addition, many of the Professional Group's paramedics and EMTs volunteer in their home towns. The Professional Group is the largest independent, privately owned ambulance provider in the state. More than 75 percent of the management and administrative staff have been care providers in the ambulance crews, which helps the entire company keep its focus on what continues to be its most important job: helping people in need.

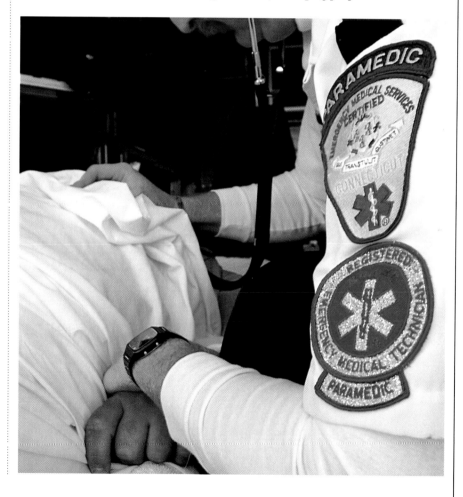

GOODWIN HOTEL

The attentive doorman at the entrance is only the beginning of the preferential service awaiting business and leisure guests at the Goodwin Hotel. Ideally located in the center of Hartford in the historic Goodwin Building, the Goodwin is the capital city's only luxury hotel.

The Goodwin's world-class accommodations include 113 elegant guest rooms and 11 luxurious suites with classic wood furnishings, marble baths, and sleigh beds, as well as valet parking, full concierge services, and an exercise facility. Modern amenities include two-line speaker telephones with computer link-up capabilities.

The Goodwin Hotel provides a range of wonderful dining experiences. Consistently rated Connecticut's best hotel restaurant, Pierpont's, the hotel's main dining room, offers a classic ambience and a varied menu of American nouveau cuisine. A bountiful brunch is served on Sundays. For cocktails and light fare, the America's Cup Lounge, with its comfortable leather chairs and wood-paneled walls, has a warm and inviting atmosphere.

Catering to the needs of business people and professionals, the Goodwin Hotel offers seven rooms well suited for meetings, conferences, and business retreats for small or large groups. The hotel's four-story Atrium can host up to 400 guests, and the professional catering staff has extensive experience in planning conventions, corporate meetings, weddings, and other special events.

Leisure travelers staying at the Goodwin benefit from the hotel's proximity to the Civic Center, varied shops and restaurants, as well as the city's many cultural venues, including the Bushnell Auditorium, the Hartford Stage Company, and the Wadsworth Atheneum, all within walking distance.

All guests and visitors of the Goodwin will appreciate the charm of its renovated and restored building, a National Historic Landmark built in 1881 by James J. and Rev. Francis Goodwin and maintained as a residence for many years by the prominent financier and Hartford native J. P. Morgan. The hotel is on Goodwin Square and adjoins the 30-story Goodwin Square Office Tower and a 302-space parking garage.

A member of Sterling Hotels and Resorts, an international association of exclusive, privately owned hotels, the Goodwin Hotel has provided luxury accommodations and impeccable service since 1989 to Hartford's most discerning guests.

© Timothy Becker

The Goodwin Hotel, built in 1881, is registered as a National Historic Landmark.

Courtesy of Goodwin Hotel

Pierpont's Restaurant has been voted "Best Hotel Dining" in Connecticut for the past six years.

FOXWOODS RESORT CASINO

© Gary J. Thibeault, CPP

The history of the Mashantucket Pequot Tribal Nation, "the Fox People," is one of great hardship, enduring spirit, and cultural renaissance.

The once-powerful tribe was almost destroyed in the Massacre of 1637. The next 350 years were marked by poverty, oppression, and a determination to survive. By 1970, just two elderly women were living at Mashantucket, the "much-wooded land." One of them, Elizabeth George Plouffe, instilled in her grandson a determination to restore tribal strength and unity. That man, Richard "Skip" Hayward, became tribal chairman in 1975.

Under Hayward's leadership, the tribe won federal recognition in 1983 and opened a high-stakes bingo hall in 1986 and Foxwoods Resort Casino in 1992.

Foxwoods Resort Casino originally employed 2,300 people and covered 250,000 square feet. It has since grown to be the largest and most profitable resort casino in the western world.

Foxwoods now encompasses 1.5 million square feet and has gaming, two hotels, 16 restaurants and food outlets, 16 retail boutiques and kiosks, a high-tech theater and entertainment complex, and two showrooms that have featured such world-renowned performers as Frank Sinatra and Luciano Pavarotti.

An $80 million, 140,000-square-foot expansion, being completed in April 1996, will include the only smoke-free gaming facility in the eastern United States. Further expansion, slated for 1998, includes a 17-story hotel, which will have 917 guest rooms as well as increased meeting and conference facilities and 60,000 square feet of additional casino space.

Foxwoods is just one of several enterprises owned and operated by the Mashantucket Pequot Tribe, which now employs more than 11,000 people, including 10,000 at Foxwoods. The tribe is among the top five employers in Connecticut.

The Mashantucket Pequot Tribe is the state's largest single-revenue provider after the federal government and is expected to pay the state more than $150 million in fiscal year 1995 under a slot revenue-sharing agreement. Each of Connecticut's 169 cities and towns receives a share of the money.

The tribe's desire to share its success with the community at large is evidenced by its major charitable contributions, including a donation of $2 million to the 1995 Special Olympics World Games.

A $150 million Mashantucket Pequot Museum and Research Center, currently under construction, is scheduled to open in 1997.

Foxwoods' success has enabled the tribe to purchase back tribal lands and to provide its members with jobs, high-quality housing, and education. Foxwoods' success has not only restored the strength and unity of the Mashantucket Pequot Tribal Nation but has proved to be a driving force in the economic growth of the state of Connecticut.

AVON OLD FARMS HOTEL, FARMINGTON INN, AND SIMSBURY INN

Nestled in the heart of the scenic and historic Farmington River Valley are three lovely sister hotels that combine country elegance with personalized professional service: the Avon Old Farms Hotel, the Farmington Inn, and the Simsbury Inn. Each with individual elements of distinction, the three hotels are run by the Brighenti family, local people who for 30 years have been dedicated to providing guests with true New England hospitality. Attention to detail is a hallmark of the three hotels, as is a desire to meet all of a guest's needs.

The Avon Old Farms Hotel, at the base of Avon Mountain, is composed of several tastefully decorated sections, totaling 160 rooms. Oriental rugs, brass chandeliers, and fresh flowers bring a relaxed warmth to the lobbies and open areas, while guest rooms and suites are spacious and comfortable. More than 400 original watercolors of the Farmington Valley, painted by local artists, adorn the walls. Seasons Restaurant, renowned in its own right, offers fresh and delicious award-winning cuisine.

The Farmington Inn, conveniently situated in the heart of Farmington, offers 72 rooms tastefully decorated in traditional or country style. Framed pieces of handmade quilts, area memorabilia, and antiques enhance the inn's simple elegance. Each guest room has a recessed door bearing a logo-inscribed brass nameplate, providing the comfortable feeling of entering one's own home. A deluxe complimentary continental breakfast is served in the pleasant second-floor dining area daily.

The luxurious Simsbury Inn, located at the center of Simsbury, has the dignified gracefulness of an old-style New

England inn as well as the amenities and service of a superior hotel. Many of the 98 guest rooms and suites offer lovely views and feature French country-style furnishings. With Evergreens Restaurant, the Nutmeg Cafe, and Twigs Lounge, the inn offers several options for fine dining.

Top choices in accommodations for corporate guests with business to conduct in the Greater Hartford area, the Avon Old Farms Hotel, the Farmington Inn, and the Simsbury Inn serve as delightful seminar and meeting locations not far from the city. With their dramatic curving staircases, gazebos, and tastefully landscaped lawns, the hotels are also popular locations for weddings and other social functions throughout the year.

For 120 years, consumers in Connecticut have had to deal with a monopoly in the local telephone market. TCG is changing that. Just as the company has done in 25 other markets across the country, TCG offers Connecticut businesses a choice in local telecommunications through the deployment of a statewide, advanced fiber-optics-based network.

In just its first year, TCG built a 300+-mile fiber-optic network that provides service from Hartford to Middletown, Waterbury, Windsor, Cheshire, and Waterford. The network is rapidly expanding to serve New Haven, Stamford, Manchester, and all other parts of the state.

By offering business consumers superior services and more service providers and by enabling communities to attract new industries today and create more opportunities tomorrow, TCG is making the benefits of local telecommunications service competition a reality. And by enhancing today's telecommunications infrastructure, TCG is creating the platform for the delivery of even greater choices to come from the emerging Information Superhighway.

TCG's private lines offer users what they don't get from the local phone company: choice, flexibility, redundancy, and the TCG commitment to anticipate and satisfy customer needs and provide tailor-made solutions.

Based on fiber-optics, a more secure, disaster-proof medium than standard copper cable, TCG's private line service has set an industry benchmark for performance by delivering an unmatched 99.99 percent availability. This remarkable statistic means the average user experiences less than three minutes of service outage per year.

TCG offers different types of private lines that operate at different speeds and that handle varying amounts of traffic in accordance with the customer's needs.

TCG offerings include:

DSO—A private line service that accommodates the basics of everyday business communications, such as telephones, fax machines, and personal computers.

DS1—For customers who need a larger communications pipeline, TCG offers this high-capacity service used to build corporate "backbone" networks. Used for voice transmissions, as well as the interconnection of local area networks (LANs), DS1 service accommodates data transmission speeds that are the equivalent of 24 voice-grade circuits.

DS3—High-capacity DS3 service permits data transmission rates that are the equivalent of 28 DS1 circuits or 672 voice-grade circuits.

European-Standard DS1 (El)—TCG was the first, and in many markets is still the only, U.S. provider to offer this private line service, which allows customers to accommodate their international traffic at unusually high speeds.

Omnilink—A standard Optical Carrier product for those companies requiring enhanced network survivability, advanced network architectures, and centralized network monitoring capabilities. Companies in many industries cannot afford the risk associated with downtime due to cable cuts, wire center/central office outages, and the like.

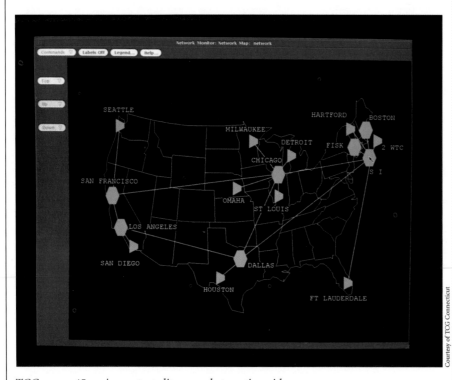

TCG serves 45 major metropolitan markets nationwide.

Courtesy of TCG Connecticut

TCG's data service, LANLINK, is used to connect workstations and PC users on one or more LANS. With LANLINK, users can share files and databases as if they were all working on the same computer. LANLINK eliminates delays or bottlenecks by allowing data transmissions to take place as fast as the network's capacity permits.

TCG switched services include:

TCG Centrex—Because TCG owns, houses, manages, and maintains the switch, customers are able to avoid unproductive investments in space, capital, and personnel that would be necessary with alternatives. TCG Centrex represents a liberating, future-ready solution that enables customers to focus resources on their business rather than on telecommunications.

TCG TeleXpress Service—Allows customers with their own PBX switches to access TCG's local network and their choice of long-distance carrier.

TCG's Extended Area Service (EAS)—A customized, high-quality local calling plan available to TCG Centrex and TCG TeleXpress customers. TCG works with clients to devise cost-saving EAS programs based on actual usage and calling needs.

TCG also supplies point-to-point, broadcast-quality video channels between two or more locations.

"Our mission is simple," says Keith Hall, Connecticut vice president and general manager. "Strengthen Connecticut's overall telecommunications infrastructure by satisfying customer requirements that are unserved or underserved by the local telephone monopoly."

Toward that end, TCG has invested millions of dollars in building SONET networks. The company has also created jobs and participated heavily in various social and charitable foundations in the

TCG's state-of-the-art networks are 100 percent fiber-optics based.

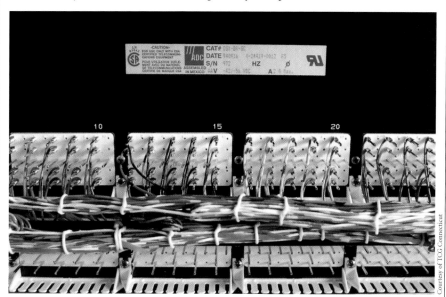

TCG, the nation's largest provider of competitive local telecommunications services, utilizes state-of-the-art switching equipment and facilities to operate as the "The Other Local Phone Company ℠" across the country.

spirit of giving something back to the community. TCG has sponsored families of children with cancer so they could go to Camp Sunshine. TCG is an active sponsor of the Canon Greater Hartford Open. And TCG employees participate in "America Care" programs by donating time to refurbish homes of impoverished elderly families.

Reliable, responsive, innovative. For more than a decade, TCG has staked its reputation on those qualities, and as a result it has taken its place as the nation's largest provider of competitive local telecommunications service.

CONNECTICUT NATURAL GAS CORPORATION

ounded in 1848 as the Hartford City Gas Light Company, Connecticut Natural Gas Corporation's (NYSE symbol CTG) growth and success have been interwoven with the growth of Greater Hartford. CTG's underground natural gas delivery system literally threads together Hartford's neighborhoods and the surrounding suburbs into a diverse but single community.

Industrial and commercial enterprises are linked to Greater Hartford by the natural gas lines that serve them. Since 18th-century entrepreneurs began to harness the power of the region's rivers, the sustaining lifeblood of New England industry has always been energy. CTG's business is pumping that lifeblood into Greater Hartford's system to serve customers, large and small, so as to keep industry producing and commerce profitable.

Today, CTG is the largest distributor of natural gas in Connecticut and serves 140,000 customers in the Greater Hartford/New Britain areas and in Greenwich. The corporation's nonregulated subsidiary, Energy Networks, Inc., provides district heating and cooling to most large buildings in downtown Hartford and the capitol area. CTG's interest in the Iroquois Gas Transmission System is held by ENI Transportation Company, another CTG subsidiary.

Throughout its history, CTG has been a model of stability, financial strength, and firm management. The company has the distinction of paying quarterly cash dividends for 144 consecutive years, longer than any other public utility listed on the New York Stock Exchange. Working together with residential customers, businesses, and industry, local and

state government, and other members of the natural gas industry, CTG continues to build the partnerships that have enabled the company to grow and prosper over the years.

CTG's future as a corporation is based on continuing to build successful partnerships with both its residential and commercial/industrial customers; with other businesses; with government, to bring the state's economy back to health; and with shareholders, to give them an honest return for their investment. "It is vital to CTG's future that Connecticut's economy continue to revive," says Victor H. Frauenhofer, CTG's chairman, president, and chief executive officer. Through conservation grants, a proactive role in community revitalization, and responsive partnerships, CTG is helping make Connecticut the state that "thinks like a business."

FOX 61 TELEPRODUCTION CENTER

FOX 61 Teleproduction Center is the award-winning production arm of FOX 61 WTIC Television in Hartford. FOX 61 Teleproduction Center has been providing video services and facilities to a variety of corporate, commercial, and independent program producers, advertising agencies, and state agencies for more than 10 years.

FOX 61 owns and operates state-of-the-art video and audio production equipment and facilities, including two studios, electronic field production packages, five edit suites, and the Colorgraphics ARTSTAR paintbox/animation system.

The master on-line edit suite provides interformat editing of one-inch, Beta, and SP Beta videotape formats. All computer-generated graphics created using the ARTSTAR system are digitally stored or, in the case of computer animation,

recorded onto the highest quality videotape, providing first-generation quality.

Field production staff use the Sony Betacam 300 with a full complement of video and audio support gear, including color monitoring; wireless, shotgun, and stereo microphones; and a portable teleprompter. A full complement of lighting instruments completes the field package.

FOX 61 Teleproduction Center's creative and technical staff are industry professionals in broadcast and corporate television. Their work has been recognized numerous times by such prestigious organizations as the Academy for Television Arts and Sciences, with Emmy awards and the Associated Press video awards, and at the New York Film Festival. Most recently, FOX 61 Teleproduction Center was recognized nationally with the bronze Telly award for "Best Documentary."

The company's customers include everyone with a need for professional, creative, high-quality video production delivered on time and within budget. FOX 61 Teleproduction Center has produced over 1,000 hours of high-quality video product, including 30-second commercials; full-length broadcast programs; corporate training and marketing tapes; video annual reports; satellite video conferencing from and to hundreds of locations around the country; new product launch videos; children's videos; "how-to" tapes; new employee orientation tapes; adult and collegiate instructional tapes; and countless other commercial, broadcast, and corporate projects.

From its studios in downtown Hartford, FOX 61 Teleproduction Center looks forward to providing continuing video support and production services to an ever-increasing family of customers here and around the country.

Courtesy of FOX 61 Teleproduction Center

THE CONNECTICUT LIGHT AND POWER COMPANY

At first glance, it may not seem as though the new International Skating Center of Connecticut, located in Simsbury, and the foundry of Philbrick-Booth & Spencer in Hartford have much in common. They're unique businesses—one hosts international celebrity skaters; the other produces high-quality steel castings. But they do share this: both own new competitive, energy-efficient operations as a result of a strong partnership with The Connecticut Light and Power Company (CL&P).

When officials of the new skating center chose to power their refrigeration system with electricity, they selected an energy option that will help ensure the center's future as an exciting new enterprise for the local economy. The same goes for the local foundry operation.

CL&P's energy management experts recommended a new electric process that allows the foundry to reclaim 80 percent of the 200 tons of sand used monthly and then to dispose of this reused sand in an environmentally safe manner. That meant the foundry could stay in business in Hartford and continue its long association with the region and the state of Connecticut.

CL&P has been a strong force in the Hartford area since its first steam engine and generator were used in a lighting demonstration at Hartford's Union Station in 1883 to introduce Connecticut's commercial electric service. The generator and steam engine were built for The Hartford Electric Light Company (HELCO), which was merged into Northeast Utilities' subsidiary, CL&P, in 1982.

More than a century after that demonstration, CL&P is still strongly committed to playing a pivotal role in the economic and community development activities of the Hartford region. Electric power is a critical element of today's commerce and industry. Through reliable, cost-efficient energy management, CL&P is forging solid partnerships in the communities it serves—with businesses, civic organizations, government, environmental groups, and other agencies.

One way CL&P helps customers become more successful is by sharing information about emerging electrotechnologies and new, efficient electric processes, many of which are available to help businesses modernize their operations, improve efficiency, and reduce costs. As customers' "Partner in Progress," CL&P provides superb customer service, competitive prices, and a comprehensive portfolio of products and services that can be tailored to meet the unique energy and business needs of individual customers.

As a part of Northeast Utilities, New England's largest electric utility, CL&P has a responsibility to provide safe, reliable, and reasonably priced electricity to 1.1 million customers in Connecticut. Over the years, the company has extended that responsibility far beyond the electric service it provides, into the streets, parks, schools, and people of the communities it serves. The success of CL&P's business is directly linked to the well-being of those communities. That's why the company has always provided strong financial and hands-on support to community programs.

The first generator and steam engine, built for The Hartford Electric Light Company, which was merged into Northeast Utilities' subsidiary, CL&P, in 1982.

A prime example of CL&P's commitment to the Connecticut economy is the selection of four Connecticut communities—East Hartford, New London, Simsbury, and Torrington—to participate in the Connecticut Main Street Program, a united community effort to protect, refurbish, and revitalize central business districts over four to five years. CL&P is the first private corporation in the country to sponsor a Main Street initiative as part of the nationwide Main Street revitalization program conducted by the nonprofit National Trust for Historic Preservation. In partnership with these first four communities, CL&P is providing initial funding, a fully staffed Connecticut Main Street outreach center, and other assistance to the communities. The aim is to develop strong local management teams to market and manage downtown areas in order to reduce high vacancy rates. By encouraging and supporting both redevelopment and new investment in municipalities and small businesses, CL&P is taking an important step in turning local economies around.

Through its partnerships with a wide range of community groups, CL&P is providing more resources to help more people. As a responsible, caring corporate citizen, CL&P and its employees have provided financial and other assistance, including numerous personal volunteer hours, to thousands of civic organizations and non-profit agencies over many years. The company has built strong partnerships with educational and environmental organizations, as well as with economic development and human services agencies.

CL&P will continue to do all it can to make life better in the communities it serves. Through strong partnerships,

The Power of Partnerships

the company has made a difference in the Greater Hartford region. CL&P will continue to be not only a premier provider of high-value energy and related services but, just as important, an involved corporate citizen, investing in the future of this region.

The International Skating Center of Connecticut, where a partnership between CL&P and the center resulted in this exciting new enterprise for the local economy.

SULLIVAN & LESHANE

Aggressive, innovative, experienced, tough—these are the words most often used to describe Sullivan & LeShane.

Since their founding in 1983, the Sullivan & LeShane companies have become widely respected for issue-centered government affairs, public relations, and strategic communications services. As one of the few organizations in Connecticut to offer integrated public affairs services, Sullivan & LeShane is uniquely qualified to help companies manage complex public policy matters and traditional public relations projects.

Sullivan & LeShane knows Connecticut. When Bristol-Myers Squibb, Johnson & Johnson, AT&T, Citicorp, Mirage Resorts, Education Alternatives, Safety-Kleen, Connecticut Mutual Insurance Co., and other companies have had government or public relations challenges in Connecticut, they have chosen Sullivan & LeShane. The firm also has excellent credentials in the Hartford area, representing the Greater Hartford Chamber of Commerce, the Hartford Downtown Council, and some of the area's most respected corporations and institutions.

Sullivan & LeShane Public Relations, Inc., has well-established statewide media contacts and credibility. The firm's people communicate with the state's major media outlets on a daily basis. They have built a reputation as "straight-shooters" who understand the needs of the news media and go out of their way to be a resource to reporters and editors.

Sullivan & LeShane's expertise extends into grassroots and community relations campaigns in support of client initiatives. The firm maintains proprietary lists of key opinion leaders and successfully initiates community organizing efforts to intensify public relations strategies. Staff often assist the firm's sister company, Sullivan & LeShane, Inc.—one of Connecticut's most influential lobbying firms—with complex public policy issues. Together, they form a powerful and effective resource for organizations and businesses to depend on in a delicate situation or during a crisis.

Sullivan & LeShane is accustomed to dealing with the high-profile and sometimes controversial issues that dominate the headlines of the state's newspapers and the halls of state and municipal governments. Whether it's introducing a revolutionary new idea, acting as advocates in a spirited public debate, or managing damage control after a major accident, Sullivan & LeShane has been instrumental in shaping some of the state's biggest stories.

Aggressive. Innovative. Experienced. Tough. Sullivan & LeShane gets the job done.

Gene Sheehan, Patrick Sullivan, and Patricia LeShane, the three principals of Sullivan & LeShane Public Relations

S uccess in the commercial real estate service business can only be assured by focusing on the needs of clients. At Farley Whittier Partners, understanding client needs has literally shaped the company in a way that gives the Farley Whittier team the incentive to be more responsive than any other commercial real estate firm in the region.

Since its inception in 1968, Farley Whittier Partners has engaged exclusively in commercial and industrial real estate activities, serving local, national, and international institutions. As a full-service firm, Farley Whittier Partners applies its entrepreneurial

Seated: Bill Farley; Michael Sherman. Standing: Cal Frese; John Stout, executive vice president; Robert Daglio; and Benjamin Terry. Not shown: Edward F. Heberger

energy to a broad range of commercial real estate services, including:

Leasing and sales of office, industrial, and retail properties
Asset and property management
Appraisal services
Marketing and research
Tenant representation
Corporate facilities management
Corporate and institutional consulting

In May 1994, the Farley Company joined forces with Whittier Partners of Boston, forming the largest commercial real estate services company in New England. This union provides comprehensive market coverage of the Greater Hartford, New Haven, Greater Boston, southern New Hampshire, and Rhode Island markets. In September 1995, Edward F. Heberger, MAI, CRE, and associates joined Farley Whittier Partners to form the Heberger Appraisal Consulting Division. In November 1995, Farley Whittier Partners opened a New Haven office.

In addition to regional dominance, Farley Whittier Partners is a vital member of ONCOR International, a worldwide organization of top-ranked independent commercial real estate firms dedicated to serving clients with needs in multiple locations. The ONCOR system provides in-depth knowledge of more than 200 markets—coordinated and delivered with single-source accountability.

Farley Whittier's nationally recognized staff are also active in the Society of Industrial and Office Realtors (SIOR), Counselors of Real Estate (CRE), Members of Appraisal Institute (MAI), Real Estate Finance Association (REFA),

Farley Whittier Partners is headquartered at 100 Pearl Street in Hartford.

Building Owners and Management Association (BOMA), Certified Commercial Investment Members (CCIM), and the Institute of Real Estate Management (IREM).

Farley Whittier Partners is a people-based company. Although the firm utilizes and invests in the most sophisticated technological database system and advanced methods of analysis, it believes that people create value in real estate and that experienced people do it well. Farley Whittier's success is a direct result of its ability to attract talented professionals in a competitive market and to inspire them to work on a collaborative basis.

In short, Farley Whittier Partners offers a consistent, high level of service that creates value for its commercial real estate clients.

What distinguishes a successful law firm? For Hebb & Gitlin, the answer is clear: anticipate the legal needs of clients through constant planning and market research, practice in a handful of sophisticated and complementary legal areas, train attorneys rigorously in several disciplines, and earn the respect of clients around the globe for performing creative legal work grounded in sound judgment.

Hebb & Gitlin has succeeded on an international scale by concentrating on corporate finance, business workouts and bankruptcies, commercial real estate, and business and insurance litigation. Greater Hartford represents an attractive home base, where, through the use of advanced technology, Hebb & Gitlin attorneys can enjoy both the challenge of a "Wall Street" practice and the quality of a New England lifestyle. The firm's reputation and client base have grown over the years to the point where its major competition is primarily from New York, Chicago, and London firms.

The firm's clients include nearly every major U.S. insurance company, several money center banks, commercial finance companies, fund managers and "nontraditional" lenders and investors, and numerous foreign financial institutions. These clients come to Hebb & Gitlin for high-end problem solving. Most of the time, the solution results because Hebb & Gitlin attorneys are able to think meaningfully in more than one area of the law.

The firm's emphasis on client service, strategic planning, and market positioning is demonstrated by its leadership role in high-profile legal projects, such as an effort by the leading insurance companies in the private placement industry to simplify and standardize investment documents and covenants, and the United Nations-sponsored Commission on International Trade Law to draft model legislation for resolving cross-border insolvencies.

Each year, the firm brings institutional investors from around the world to Hartford for the "Hebb & Gitlin Institute" to study the legal and practical implications of the latest international investment trends with experts in finance, insolvency, and accounting.

Ed Hebb and Richard Gitlin founded the firm in 1973 based on a simple formula for success: plan for the future, cross-train attorneys, and nurture entrepreneurial spirit. Another core value they wanted embodied in their firm was a spirit of caring for others who are less fortunate. People at Hebb & Gitlin recognize their responsibility to share their success with the community where they live and work. The Connecticut Bar Association has honored the firm for its pro bono activities. In addition, employees participate in a variety of charitable fund-raising events each year throughout the Hartford area.

Courtesy of Hebb & Gitlin

Ed Hebb (left) and Richard Gitlin founded their law firm in 1973 based on a few simple principles: plan for the future, cross-train attorneys, and nurture entrepreneurial spirit.

VALERIE E. THOMAS, CLU CHARTERED FINANCIAL CONSULTANT AND ASSOCIATES, LLC

Financial security. Two simple but powerful words describing what for some is life's pursuit, while for others a hopeless dream. Yet many people achieve their financial goals and retire comfortably, even without having amassed a fortune during their working years. Their secret: good planning, expert guidance, and discipline.

"There are dozens of ways to save for retirement. It's simply a matter of creating a plan that meets your personal needs and then planning the steps you'll need to take to achieve your goals," says Valerie E. Thomas, chartered life underwriter and chartered financial consultant.

Valerie E. Thomas, CLU Chartered Financial Consultant and Associates, located on the Silas Deane Highway in Wethersfield, provides estate and retirement planning and specializes in helping individuals and families develop and implement financial plans customized to suit their particular needs.

"It's not enough to help families realize their financial dreams, or to help businesspeople achieve their economic goals," Thomas says. "Life can be hard, and you have to stay ahead of it by making sound judgments based on experience and common sense and using the variety of tools and saving mechanisms available. My job is to ensure that our clients can care for their families and businesses in good times and bad."

"The major challenges of estate planning are minimizing probate problems and reducing estate taxes," says Thomas. "We help our clients to preserve their estates and ensure the assets

Valerie and Norman Thomas (center) discuss legal contracts with members of the Connecticut Estate and Tax Planning Council, Inc., Kenneth T. Kelley (left) and John F. Kearns III (right).

are distributed according to their wishes." The firm annually saves clients millions of dollars in estate taxes.

Valerie Thomas has been in the financial planning field since 1973, assisting owners, employees, and retirees of large and small companies and nonprofit organizations to achieve financial stability and comfort. Well known in the industry, she also serves as Securities Principal for the State of Connecticut for Sun Investment Services, a subsidiary of Sun Life of Canada, and is a member of the Connecticut Estate and Tax Planning Council.

In addition to private consulting, the firm offers a variety of workshops and seminars on estate and retirement planning, investments, family protection, business planning, pension plans, taxes, and long-term care.

DAY, BERRY & HOWARD

With more than 210 lawyers, Day, Berry & Howard is Connecticut's largest and most successful law firm. On four floors of Hartford's CityPlace, the firm's lawyers handle complex legal matters for a full range of clients—from individuals to closely held private enterprises to companies listed on the New York Stock Exchange. Founded in Hartford in 1919, the firm opened full-service offices in Stamford during 1978 and in Boston during 1981.

While the firm's practice has expanded to many new areas, Day, Berry & Howard continues to excel in litigation and business law, which have been the foundations of its practice. Day, Berry & Howard has the broadest litigation practice in New England and one of the region's most sophisticated finance practices.

In response to the needs of an evolving business environment, Day, Berry & Howard has developed practice areas in many legal disciplines, including product liability, environmental law, international transactions, securities and securities litigation, employee benefits and employment law, government regulation, health care, intellectual property, state tax litigation, and governmental investigations. In addition, the firm continues to provide advice on administrative and regulatory law, creditors' rights and bankruptcy, insurance litigation, ERISA, estate planning and probate litigation, family law, real estate transactions, and federal income taxation.

Day, Berry & Howard consistently demonstrates its commitment to the local community. Lawyers and support staff hold positions of leadership in many civic, community, and governmental organizations. Each lawyer is required to perform at least 50 hours of community work annually, and many give much more. The firm also has a distinguished record of pro bono service to the community in the courtroom.

Quality, innovation, and teamwork characterize Day, Berry & Howard. Quality means providing clients with superior sophisticated advice. Innovation speaks of the firm's creative yet practical solutions to real-world problems. And, finally, teamwork characterizes the firm's ability to assemble a multidisciplined team of lawyers who work effectively with each other and with the firm's clients. It is the combination of all three, every day, in every matter, that sets Day, Berry & Howard apart.

Day, Berry & Howard has a distinguished record of providing pro bono work in the courtroom and in the form of community service. Partners, associates, and staff volunteered to create a beautiful playground, including a tire playscape, for the children in the Hartford Region YWCA Childcare Program.

Founded in 1932 during the depths of the Depression by the Sisters of Mercy, Saint Joseph College was established to provide the daughters of working-class families with access to excellence in higher education. Hartford was experiencing a recession of its own in 1991 when Winifred Coleman arrived as president and took on the college's

first capital campaign. "People were amazed that we would undertake the campaign in the face of such severe economic difficulty," said President Coleman, "but I thought this couldn't be any more challenging than the situation our founders faced. So we moved ahead, and, with the help of many, we accomplished our goal." The results of that campaign include the renovation of such major campus facilities as the library reference room, the nursing learning center, and the physical science/education laboratory; the con-

struction of The O'Connell Athletic Center; and the improved accessibility of the main academic building for persons with disabilities.

Faith and foresight continue to be hallmarks of Saint Joseph College. "As Connecticut's only four-year women's college, we are dedicated to developing women leaders," says Executive Vice President Maureen Reardon, R.S.M. "Here, in an atmosphere that is both rigorous and embracing, our students learn to use all of their faculties—intellectual, emotional, physical, and spiritual—to the fullest. We are fostering skills traditionally considered feminine, such as networking and team-building, at a time when employers have identified them as essential to success in the global marketplace." International exchange

programs with Japan, India, Denmark, and Great Britain create opportunities for students to demonstrate these skills worldwide.

In addition to the Women's College,

which has been featured six consecutive times in *U.S. News & World Report* as "one of America's best," the SJC campus houses the Graduate School and the Weekend College, for women and men, the School for Young Children, and the Gengras Center, a special education facility for youth ages 3 to 21. As Provost Martin Snyder notes, "Today we serve

women and men of all ages, abilities, and backgrounds, delivering the vision the sisters began with, excellence in education while responding to the changing needs of society."

The United Way movement has been making a positive impact in this country for more than 100 years. It began in Denver, Colorado, in 1887 under the leadership of two ministers, a priest, and a rabbi who wanted to coordinate the efforts of various charitable groups. Greater Hartford's United Way, then called the Community Chest, was established in April 1924, following an intensive two-year study to assess the needs of the community. It is one of the strongest representatives of Hartford's diversity.

The study, carried out by a group of leading citizens from the city's oldest families and esteemed corporations, concluded that having one parent organization raise and distribute funds to nonprofit agencies was a more efficient way to solicit contributions from the community. Modeled after similar organizations throughout the country, the Greater Hartford Community Chest was located at 36 Trumbull Street and ran its first campaign from November 7 to November 17, 1924, from campaign headquarters at the Old State House. That very first campaign raised $380,000, exceeding the goal of $315,000. The money raised benefited 24 health and human service agencies, including some familiar names that are still serving the community today—the American Red Cross, Salvation Army, and Hartford Dispensary.

In October 1924, the *Hartford Daily Times* wrote, "By means of the chest it is believed more money will be given for those in need: more individual citizens will be interested and can devote their time to the real work of social ser-

Courtesy of United Way

vice; the cost of operation will be reduced; the generous citizen can plan his giving in relation to his income, for he will receive only one appeal in place of 24 or more; team work will be increased; and total expenditure planned in more direct relation to the community needs."

Today, these principles continue to guide the United Way, as it was renamed in 1973, and has allowed it the flexibility to meet the Greater Hartford area's continually changing needs. Since 1924, United Way has raised and distributed more than $400 million and is constantly evaluating itself so that it can address the most relevant and pressing issues each year with one basic underlying philosophy—when everyone gives, everyone benefits.

The Community Campaign, which became a joint effort with Combined Health Appeal in 1983, serves the greatest number of people in need through more than 135 agencies in the 40-town Capital Region. Experienced and committed volunteers representing all social, racial, and economic backgrounds keep the distribution process fair and ensure that contributions reach people who need help the most.

We have all been touched, or know someone who has been touched, by a United Way agency. Need is not biased. It crosses all racial and ethnic lines. The United Way is prepared to listen to and meet the needs of Greater Hartford's residents. Whether it's treating someone for an addiction or teaching youths how to prevent an addiction, we all benefit from the work done at United Way agencies. They are there to help a senior citizen get to a medical appointment. They are there to help resolve family conflicts. They are there to solve problems we face on a daily basis.

And United Way agencies are producing tangible results. For example, 87 percent of all youths at the Boys' and Girls' Clubs graduate from high school, compared with 66 percent of all youth in America. At United Labor Agency, 80 percent of the people receiving assistance found jobs. Foodshare of Greater Hartford provides food for more than 5.8 million meals each year. And 94 percent of parents participating in a Parents Anonymous group at the Connecticut Center for Prevention of Child Abuse say they now discipline their child(ren) in ways other than hitting or yelling.

The United Way develops resources for our community in the broadest sense, providing more than just dollars. From volunteers to goods and services, a wide spectrum of needs in our diverse community is served. From the heart of the Frog Hollow neighborhood to the city's downtown streets to the surrounding suburbs, the United Way of the Capital Region is insuring a brighter future for the Hartford area.

Founded in Hartford in 1823, Trinity College is one of the nation's oldest colleges and is consistently ranked among its finest undergraduate liberal arts colleges. Trinity is noted for:

- its excellent instruction, which is personal and conversational, with a student/faculty ratio of 10 to 1;
- its rigorous pursuit of study in the liberal arts and sciences; and
- its ability to reap the educational advantages of its city setting.

Trinity draws its 1,750 students from 47 states and 24 countries. Admission is highly competitive, with more than six applicants for each place in the freshman class. Trinity also offers a graduate studies program and an individualized degree program for adults seeking a bachelor's degree.

Trinity's presence and impact are evident in many ways in Hartford and the nation.

Economic vitality. The college contributes nearly $100 million annually to the economic health of Hartford and its metropolitan area.

Intellectual enrichment. More than 1,000 campus events occur annually. Many are open to the public: student and visiting artist performances and exhibits at the Austin Arts Center; lectures by scholars and leaders; first-rate films at Cinestudio; a summer carillon and chamber music series; and Division III sports.

Trinity's library collections are substantial for a small college and, in some areas, rank with those of university libraries. Its rare book and archival resources in the Watkinson Library include a prominent collection of early printed books, primary source material for the study of 19th-century social history (both American and British), and the ornithology collection of Ostrom and Alice Enders.

Proven outcomes. A national survey ranked Trinity third among undergraduate colleges in producing corporate executives. Half of all undergraduates complete at least one internship prior to graduation.

Recognized scholarship. Faculty and alumni have won 11 coveted Pulitzer Prizes, a record that few liberal arts colleges have achieved.

Innovation. The National Science Foundation has cited Trinity as an "exemplar institution" for extensive, innovative uses of computing.

High standards. Trinity is one of two highly selective liberal arts colleges whose bachelor of science degree in engineering carries the professional certification of the national Accreditation Board for Engineering and Technology.

Partners with Hartford. More than 800 students and faculty volunteer annually in college-sponsored community service, contributing more than 10,000 hours of service. The college opens its campus to community groups, especially those dedicated to area youths.

Worldly connections. Trinity's campus in Rome, its study program in Spain, and its domestic study program, Trinity/LaMama Performing Arts in New York City, are among many learning options available to students. More than 40 percent study abroad for a semester or a year in more than 30 countries on six continents.

Courtesy of Trinity College

Northam Towers on Trinity College's Long Walk, a series of adjoining brownstones that was modeled after the architecture of Cambridge and Oxford universities in England

In a city devoted to the celebration of cultural diversity, the Hartford Public Library excels as an institution committed to providing the informational resources required by a changing, multicultural population. With over half a million books, the library is the largest in Connecticut. But it is much more than a repository for books and printed literature. Indeed, it may be more appropriate to think of it as a multimedia center.

Under the guidance of Louise Blalock, chief librarian, this 100-year-old institution continues to expand its holdings to meet the library service and information needs of everyone who lives and works in Hartford, including the requirements of an increasingly electronic-based culture. The library has a large and expanding multimedia collection—videos, CDs, and books on tape. It also provides customers with computer links to the Information Superhighway, as well as a wealth of worldwide databases.

Beyond the central library at 500 Main Street, the library has nine branches and a bookmobile that serve every Hartford neighborhood and offer unique collections that address the heritage and cultural needs of each community.

Customers also benefit from the fact that the library is at the center of a network of libraries serving every town in the Greater Hartford area. Connected by computers and telecommunications, the libraries in the system can access each other's databases, giving all customers the maximum potential to obtain the information and resources they seek.

Blalock believes the library should serve as a cultural resource in the broadest sense. Throughout the year, the central library presents concerts by an unusually diverse range of musicians. During fall and winter months, the concerts are held inside. In the summer, the public is invited every Thursday to enjoy live music and dancing on the terrace. The library holds poetry slams and brings authors to speak to large audiences. A variety of programs for children and adults are regular happenings at both the central library and the branches.

In a community whose revitalization and growth depend on information and ideas, the Hartford Public Library is a capital resource.

Summer on the terrace at the Hartford Public Library

THE HARTFORD CLUB

The Hartford Club of today, and for more than 120 years, has been recognized as a place to gather in friendship and camaraderie. The sentiment shared by the men and women of this club is best expressed by the following statement taken from the venerable St. Andrews Club of Scotland:

A CLUB

Is a haven of refuge and accord in a world torn by strive and discord;

Is a place where kindred spirits gather to have fun and make friends;

Is a place of courtesy, good breeding and good manners;

Is a place expressly for camaraderie, merriment, good will and good cheer;

It humbles the mighty, draws out the timid, and casts out the sorehead;

And is one of the noblest inventions of mankind!

The Hartford Club's long tradition of leadership in commerce, government, and society stands at the core of the Greater Hartford community. Today, however, the membership is drawn as often from new emerging entrepreneurial ventures as from Fortune 500 corporations.

The diversity of the current member population is a reflection of the changes in Hartford—and the country—as business ownership has shifted from traditional multilayered corporations to individuals. These days the independent

and the corporate member stand side by side, taking advantage of the unique opportunities for fellowship and goodwill that continue to be the common thread, as they have been from the opening days, at the Hartford Club.

On any given day, one experiences the energy that moves through the stately rooms as members and their guests gather for business and social times; and holding court over all this activity are the former and formidable club presidents, whose photographs portray the heritage of the Hartford Club.

To appreciate the impact of the Hartford Club on the Greater Hartford community both historically and economically, one must read *The Club on Prospect Street—A History of The Hartford Club* by Ellsworth S. Grant, a Connecticut historian. Commissioned by the board of governors of the club and published in 1984, "This text examines the club movement and traces the

evolution of the club tradition in this country, in Connecticut, and in Hartford." As stated in the publication's preface, "The Hartford Club is, in many ways, the history of Hartford. Here, some of New England's most influential people have lived, taken their leisure and held conversations that shaped the city, state and region."

No discourse on the Hartford Club would be complete without the mention of one of its famous and favorite sons, Mark Twain, whose unique personality left an enduring mark in literature, politics, and society.

Constructed in 1903 and an outstanding example of Georgian revival design, the Hartford Club claimed a place on the National Register of Historic Places as "carefully detailed and well proportioned in a sophisticated manner." It was designed by the Boston architectural firm of Andrews, Jacques & Ranford. Robert D. Andrews also was a native of Hartford.

Since 1957, when Hillyer College, the Hartford Art School, and the Hartt School combined to form one institution, the University of Hartford has grown from a relatively small, nonresidential university to one that represents the diversity of the local and world communities.

The university's suburban 320-acre campus is home to more than 4,000 undergraduates. The university also offers comprehensive educational programs through its nine schools and colleges: the Hartford Art School, the Hartt School, Hartford College for Women, the College of Arts and Sciences, Hillyer College, the College of Engineering, the Barney School of Business and Public Administration, the Ward College of Technology, and the College of Education, Nursing, and Health Professions. Students are able to choose from more than 70 undergraduate majors and more than 50 graduate degree programs.

But the vastness of the university's programs does not mean its students face the anonymity of big-campus life. In fact, the university promotes small class sizes and face-to-face interaction.

Cooperative education and internship placements enable students to develop job skills and gain work experience. An honors program, independent study, cross-registration at area colleges, and opportunities to study abroad all enhance the range of the academic experience.

While many colleges are faulted for their weak town-gown relations, the University of Hartford is well utilized by the Hartford community. Its sports center is home to 18 Division I teams, while the Harry Jack Gray Center holds a comprehensive library, the Joseloff Gallery, TV and radio studios, a bookstore, and the university's Museum of American Political Life. The university's radio station, WWUH, has long been appreciated by local listeners for its innovative music and informative programming.

The university also serves the Greater Hartford community in other ways. In the past few years, it has launched new degree programs geared to the local economy. A business and industry initiative is designed to make the university's extensive resources more available to the region's corporate community. And the university's Downtown Center, at 99 Pratt Street, is more than just a place of learning; it is part of the revitalization of the city.

From its students to the businesses that are the backbone of the regional economy, the University of Hartford is committed to excellence in education and excellence in service.

© Robert A. _isak

The University of Connecticut is a rich resource for citizens of the state. Each year, it offers some 25,000 students at 10 campuses more than 90 undergraduate majors and professional programs in social work, law, medicine, business, and dental medicine.

The University was founded in 1881 as the Storrs Agricultural School. It became a university in 1939, granted its first doctoral degrees in 1949, and is a Land Grant, Sea Grant, and Space Grant Consortium institution. The University contributes to the state's quality of life through its teaching, research, cultural programs, and public service performed by its faculty, staff, and students and by the more than the 90,000 alumni who live in Connecticut.

UConn is considered a "Public Ivy" and is ranked among the top 35 universities in the nation by the National Science Foundation. The Carnegie Foundation classifies UConn with only five other institutions in the Northeast as a Class I research institution. Among the strongest programs are biological sciences, materials science, psychology, nutritional sciences, pharmacy, physics, history, marine sciences, electrical and systems engineering, linguistics, puppetry, and gifted education.

UConn's two largest campuses are the Storrs campus, with 4,400 acres and 193 major buildings, and the Health Center in Farmington, with 151 acres and the John Dempsey Hospital. The University's libraries have the largest public collection of materials in the state. UConn's Jorgensen Auditorium, School of Fine Arts, and Homer Babbidge Library provide cultural events

for the region, including theater, music, and art. The Thomas J. Dodd Research Center, The William Benton Museum of Art, and the Connecticut State Museum of Natural History are located on the Storrs campus.

The University of Connecticut entered a significant new era in 1995 with the enactment of the UConn 2000 legislation. UConn 2000 establishes a structured 10-year, $1 billion program to rebuild the University's infrastructure at

the Storrs campus, as well as to construct and equip academic and research facilities in Storrs and at the regional campuses (Stamford, Avery Point, Hartford, Torrington, and Waterbury). The law also establishes a matching grants program, similar to programs at other public universities, designed to encourage and reward UConn's efforts to increase substantially the level of private donations from alumni, corporations, and others.

Undergraduate students outside the Wilbur Cross Building on the University of Connecticut Storrs campus

Many sports fans yearn for simpler days and the notion of competing for the sheer love of the game.

The new management behind Hartford's major league franchise, KTR Hockey Limited Partnership, took ownership of the Hartford Whalers in June of 1994. Where they come from, love of the game is alive and well.

The Whalers' front office combines NHL experience with years developing talent at the junior level.

Chief Executive Officer Peter Karmanos founded Compuware, one of the fastest-growing software corporations in the world. With the fruits of his computer software company's success, Karmanos lent corporate sponsorship to youth hockey, culminating in his Ontario Hockey League (OHL) Windsor Spitfires reaching the Memorial Cup finals in 1988.

In 1989, Karmanos and his group were granted an OHL expansion franchise for Detroit. The first American team in the history of that league, it became the Detroit Junior Whalers in 1995.

Whalers president and general manager Jim Rutherford, as director of hockey operations for Compuware Sports Corporation, coached the 1988 Spitfires. He went on to lead the Detroit OHL entry to its first-ever playoff berth.

As a mentor to young talent, Rutherford knew whereof he spoke. For 13 seasons he tended goal in the National Hockey League (NHL) for the Penguins, Maple Leafs, Kings, and Red Wings.

Newly installed head coach Paul Maurice also brings OHL junior hockey coaching experience to the Whalers. And at age 28, his presence behind the bench promises a dynamic new outlook.

The Whalers organization is not just developing hockey's next generation in their original home base of Detroit. There is also a Junior Whalers, headquartered in Enfield, Connecticut, and a Connecticut Midget Whalers, for boys ages 15 to 17, in Simsbury.

Two years ago, the Whalers joined Nike and the NHL to launch "Street Whalers," a grassroots program that allows city kids to get a first taste of hockey—in sneakers.

The "For Kids' Skate" program sets youngsters up with ice skates and ice time at the Hartford Civic Center to teach them the game.

Cities larger than Hartford may have three or four big league teams involved in good works in the community. The Whalers more than make up for any slack by their involvement in over 30 local charities—most prominently the UConn Children's Cancer Fund.

The Greater Hartford Jaycees is an organization of young men and women between the ages of 21 and 39. The Jaycees offers members the opportunity to meet new people, develop leadership and personal skills, and contribute to society.

Founded in 1944, the Greater Hartford Jaycees boasts more than 500 members, a foundation for giving grants and scholarships, and the Canon Greater Hartford Open (GHO), a PGA Tour Golf Tournament, as its sole fund-raiser.

Opportunities for individual growth include positions on the chapter or foundation board of directors, planning the Canon GHO, and chairing chapter-sponsored projects. Projects run by the Greater Hartford Jaycees include providing holiday gifts for abused and neglected children, giving Thanksgiving turkeys to needy Hartford residents, outings for special citizens, and training programs for chapter members.

The Greater Hartford Jaycees Foundation, the grant-giving entity of the chapter, seeks to promote the quality of life for Greater Hartford residents. This is done by awarding grants to nonprofit organizations and scholarships to high school seniors.

Established in 1970, the foundation has awarded over $10 million to programs benefiting the area's children, elderly, disabled, and disadvantaged. Typical programs funded by the foundation provide medical care for low-income families, help prevent domestic and gang violence, provide low-income housing, and build self-esteem in inner-city youth.

The Canon Greater Hartford Open is the premier sporting event in New England. Each year the world's best golfers come to Connecticut to take on the Tournament Players Club at River Highlands, one of the most challenging courses on the PGA Tour. Enormous spectator galleries continually rank the Canon GHO one of the largest events on the tour. The list of past tournament champions reads like a who's who of golf: Arnold Palmer, Lee Trevino, Dave Stockton, Paul Azinger, Nick Price, and Greg Norman, to name a few. In 1973, Sammy Davis, Jr., became involved and lent his name and talents to the tournament for over a decade. In 1985, Canon USA became the title sponsor. One year later, the tournament was moved to the Tournament Players Club in Cromwell, Connecticut, where it is still held each summer.

But the Canon GHO is about more than blue skies, green fairways, and the roar of the crowd. Since 1952, the Greater Hartford Jaycees have operated the tournament as their sole fund-raiser to support the works of the chapter and the foundation. Thousands of volunteers turn out each year to help the Jaycees run this popular event, truly making it a community effort and helping make winners of us all.

The Canon GHO, New England's premier sporting event, is the sole fund-raiser for the Greater Hartford Jaycees.

ACKNOWLEDGMENTS

Each of the following organizations, health-care and educational institutions, and government entities made a valuable contribution to this project. Longstreet Press gratefully acknowledges their participation:

Aetna Life and Casualty Company
Avon Old Farms Hotel, Farmington Inn, and
    Simsbury Inn
B. Perkins & Co., Inc.
Bradley International Airport and Signature
    Flight Support
ConnectiCare
Connecticut Capitol Region Growth Council and
    Connecticut Economic Resource Center, Inc.
Connecticut Children's Medical Center
Connecticut Institute for the Blind/Oak Hill
Connecticut Light and Power Company
Connecticut Natural Gas Corporation
City of Hartford
Coopers & Lybrand
Day, Berry & Howard
Farley Whittier Partners
Fleet Bank
FOX 61 Teleproduction Center
Foxwoods Resort Casino
Goodwin Hotel
Greater Hartford Chamber of Commerce
Greater Hartford Jaycees
Hartford Club
Hartford Hospital
Hartford Public Library
Hartford Steam Boiler Inspection and
    Insurance Company
Hartford Whalers
HealthChoice of Connecticut
Hebb & Gitlin
Heublein Inc.
Holiday Inn Hartford-Downtown
Hospital for Special Care
Institute of Living
ITT Hartford
Loctite Corporation
Oxford Health Plans
P/A Industries
Phoenix
Professional Group
Residence Inn by Marriott
Saint Francis Hospital and Medical Center
Saint Joseph College
Simscroft-Echo Farms
Sullivan & LeShane
TCG Connecticut
Travelers Insurance
Trinity College
United Way
University of Connecticut
University of Connecticut Health Center
University of Hartford
Valerie E. Thomas, CLU Chartered Financial
    Consultant and Associates, LLC
Wiremold Company

The Greater Hartford Chamber of Commerce would like to thank all of those who contributed to the publication of *Greater Hartford: Celebrating Cultural Diversity.*

Those who voluntarily helped to promote the project include:

Michael P. Peters, Mayor, City of Hartford
Thomas J. Groark, Jr., Chairman, Greater
    Hartford Chamber of Commerce Board of
    Directors, and partner, Day, Berry & Howard
Mary Hart, member, Greater Hartford Chamber
    of Commerce, and Director, Public Relations,
    Connecticut Natural Gas Company

Staff who dedicated their time and efforts to the project include:

Sharon Brown, Director, Member Services
Anthony M. Caruso, Senior Vice President,
    Chamber Services
Joseph Ierna, Senior Vice President, Programs and
    Public Policy
Joann Lombardo, Director, Public Affairs
Daniel Moors, Senior Director, Public Affairs
Timothy J. Moynihan, President, Greater Hartford
    Chamber of Commerce
Kim Sirois, Project Manager and Assistant Director,
    Communications

The Greater Hartford Chamber of Commerce would also like to thank Jim Smith and photographer Lanny Nagler, who went above and beyond the call of duty to capture Greater Hartford as a wonderful place in which to live, work, and visit. They truly uncovered Hartford's many secrets and treasures. We hope this exclusive publication will open many eyes to what we have here in this rare, historic city of ours.

The following individuals and organizations were excellent sources of information for the text:

Carol Atlas
Gino Avenoso, Franklin Avenue and South End
    Merchants Association
Joe Bordenaro, Franklin Avenue and South End
    Merchants Association
Jim Boucher, HART
Art Brodeur, University of Connecticut
Jonathon Bruce, CRT Craftery
Steve Campo, TheaterWorks
Keith Carr, Upper Albany Merchants Association
Ted Carroll, Leadership Greater Hartford
John Chapin, Gov. John Rowland's office
Larry Charles, One-Chane
Ryland Charronsmith
Maureen Connolly, Maureen Connolly Management
Dr. Leslie Cutler, President, University of
    Connecticut Health Center

Dr. David D'Eramo, President, Saint Francis/Mount
    Sinai Health Care System
Mayor Robert DeCrescenzo, East Hartford
Dr. Evan Dobelle, Trinity College
Chief Robert Dobson, Hartford Fire Department
Larry Dorman
Lee Erdmann, Town Manager, Wethersfield
Bill Faude, Old State House
Gary Frank
Anthony Giorgio, Connecticut Capitol Region
    Growth Council
Judy Green, Artworks Gallery
Robb Hankins, Greater Hartford Arts Council
Austin Jordan, Hartford Guides
Anthony Keller, Charter Oak Cultural Center
Michael Kerski, Greater Hartford Architecture
    Conservancy
Mayor Sandy Klebanoff, West Hartford
Knox Parks Foundation
Alan Levy, Hartford Children's Theatre
Rev. Cornell Lewis
Diana McCain, Connecticut Historical Society
Dollie McLean, Artists Collective
Joe Marfuggi, Riverfront Recapture, Inc.
John Meehan, President, Hartford Hospital
Ira Morrison
Sue Mullaney
Deputy Chief Tom O'Connor, Hartford Police
    Department
Mark O'Donnell, Project EQUAL
Tana Parseliti, Business for Downtown Hartford
Pedro de Pedro, Spanish American Merchants
    Association
Mayor Mike Peters, Hartford
David Ransom
Phil Schenck, Town Manager, Avon
Dale Shank and Pacific Habitat Services
Marcelina Sierra, Guakia, Inc.
Dr. Ann Stuart, Hartford Graduate Center
John Wardlaw, Hartford Housing Authority
Will Wilkins, Real Art Ways
Mark Winne, Hartford Food System

The following individuals and organizations were extremely helpful in achieving the high quality of the photographs:

Fuji Film USA Inc.
Michael Simonds, Simonds Photographic
Stan White, Eastman Kodak Co.
Primary Colour Labs

$\mathcal{I}$NDEX TO ENTERPRISE SECTION